1 MONTH OF FREE READING

at

www.ForgottenBooks.com

By purchasing this book you are eligible for one month membership to ForgottenBooks.com, giving you unlimited access to our entire collection of over 1,000,000 titles via our web site and mobile apps.

To claim your free month visit:

www.forgottenbooks.com/free789989

ISBN 978-0-483-58765-6
PIBN 10789989

This book is a reproduction of an important historical work. Forgotten Books uses
state-of-the-art technology to digitally reconstruct the work, preserving the original format
whilst repairing imperfections present in the aged copy. In rare cases, an imperfection in
the original, such as a blemish or missing page, may be replicated in our edition. We do,
however, repair the vast majority of imperfections successfully; any imperfections that
remain are intentionally left to preserve the state of such historical works.

CONTENTS

MASMID—Published by the Students' Organization of Yeshiva College. Vol. I. No. 5.

Dr. BERNARD REVEL
President of the Faculty

Dr. SHELLEY R. SAFIR
Dean

FACULTY

Maurice Chazin, Ph.D...*Instructor in French*

Julius K. Littman, B.S., M.D...*Instructor in Physiology*

Ben Zion Rosenbloom, M.A...*Instructor in Psychology*

Nathan Savitsky, M.A., M.D...*Instructor in Psychology*

ASSOCIATED FACULTY

Robert C. Dickson, A.B., M.A...*English*
    Instructor in English, College of the City of New York.

Jacob Henry Landman, J.S.D., Ph.D..*History*
    Instructor in History, College of the City of New York.

Samuel A. Rutledge, M.A., Ph.D..*Education*
    Instructor, Jamaica Training College.

In recognition *of* their sincere enthusiasm *to the cause of* Yeshiva College, *we the* Student *Body,* respectfully dedicated *this our* Second Commencement *Issue to*

THE FACULTY

Bernard Revel, Ph.D.............. President
Shelley R. Safir, Ph.D.. Dean, and Professor of Biology
Pinkhos Churgin, Ph.D. .... Assoc. Prof. of Hebrew Literature
Bernard Drachman, Ph.D.. ... Instructor in German
Jekuthiel Ginsberg, M.A.. ... Assoc. Professor of Mathematics
Abraham B. Hurwitz, M.A.................................... ... Instructor in Physical Education
Moses L. Isaacs, Ph.D.d................................ .. ... ··Instructor in Chemistry
Leo Jung, Ph.D.. .. .. .. Professor of Ethics
Joseph Kahn, Ph.D.. . Instructor in Chemistry
Nathan Klotz, Ph.D............................... .. .. Instructor in Bible
Raphael Kurzrok, M.D., Ph.D.................. ... .. Lecturer in Physiology
Erastus Palmer, M.A..Professor of Public Speaking
Solomon Gandz, Ph.D.. Librarian
Joseph Glanz, B.S..Assistant in Chemistry
Joseph Ridman, B.S.................................. ... ··. Assistant Librarian

ASSOCIATED FACULTY

Kenneth F. Damon, M.A.. Public Speaking
Instructor in Public Speaking, College of the City of New York.

William J. Farma, M.A.. Public Speaking
Assistant Professor of Public Speaking, New York University.

Solomon Flink.. ... Economics
Instructor in Economics, College of the City of New York, M.A., Columbia University, 1928; Ph.D., 1930.

Henry E. Garrett, Ph.D.. ... Psychology
Assistant Professor of Psychology, Columbia University.

Charles F. Horne, Ph.D.. ..... English
Professor of English, College of the City of New York.

Solomon Liptzin, Ph.D.. German
Instructor in German, College of the City of New York.

Alexander Litman, Ph.D.. Philosophy
Instructor in Philosophy, Columbia University.

Walter C. Langsam, Ph.D.. History
Instructor in History, Columbia University.

Nelson P. Mead, Ph.D.. History
Professor of History, College of the City of New York.

Milton Offutt, Ph.D. .... History
Instructor in History, College of the City of New York.

Joseph Pearl, Ph.D.. Latin
Associate Professor of Latin, Brooklyn College, N. Y.

Isidore A. Schwartz, Ph.D.. French
Instructor in French, School of Education, C. C. N. Y.

Joseph T. Shipley, Ph.D.. English
Instructor in English, School of Education, C. C. N. Y.

Louis A. Watsoff, L.L.M., J.Sc.D..Government
Instructor in Government, Brooklyn College.

Solomon Zeitlin, Ph.D.. Jewish History
Professor of Rabbinics, Dropsie College.

CLASS OF 1933

To Alma Mater

O thou who did'st with tenderness and care
    Aid us the rocky cliffs of truth to scale,
And from the flames of youthful doubt to bear
    The spark of faith, whose light shall never fail,

To thee we raise our voice in grateful song;
    'Twixt memory and hope are built our lives,
The spirit of the East of ages long,
    Thou bringest to the West—the union thrives.

The vine's sweet fruit, the grape, can never grow
    Upon the stem of prickly pointed thorn,
Nor thistles bear, no matter who may sow,
    The fig whose juice feeds nations yet unborn.

Implanted deep thy seeds of mind and heart
    That grow as one in consummated art.

—ABRAHAM S. GUTERMAN

JACOB AGUSHEWITZ
New York City

GRAD

MEYER ESKOWITZ
New York City

PHILIP BRAND
New York City

19

UATES

ISRAEL E. FRIEDMAN
Providence, R. I.

AARON S. FEINERMAN
New York City

33

ISAAC GOLDBERG
Newark, N. J.

SIDNEY F. GREEN
New York City

GRAD

HYMAN A. ISRAEL
Waco, Texas

ABRAHAM S. GUTERMAN
Scranton, Pa.

19

UATES

SIDNEY NISSENBAUM
Jersey City, N. J.

NATHAN JOCOBSON
New York City

33

LEO PODOLSKY
New York City

HIRSCHEL E. REVEL
New York City

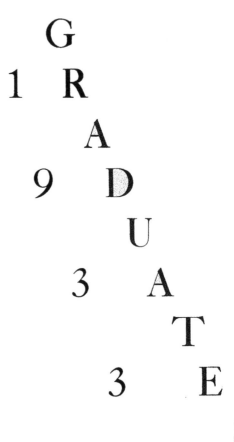

GRADUATES
1933

NORMAN REVEL
New York City

A NEW HEART

By

DR. BERNARD REVEL

In these dark and distressful days of a material and spiritual crisis in human history, when the practical and the moral fabrics are strained to the breaking point; when mankind is at the cross-roads of the spirit, bewildered, yearning for true leadership, for peace and brotherhood, groping toward an unknown destiny, seeking a new way and clearer guidance, whence are to come man's sign-posts and man's salvation, humanity's bridge over the slough of despond and present chaos? We are beginning to understand that the root of today's world distraction is moral. The times are *spiritually* out of joint. On the material plane, in this great land at least, we are being cheered by the promise, and the early indications, of "a new deal." But man's greatest need in this unprecedented crisis is, in the words of the Seer of Israel, "a new heart." The world's crying need is for a heart of understanding and compassion, begetting love and faith, the strengthening of the moral fibre, for a greater discernment of and return to the ultimate values of life, the true values of the spirit. A spiritual interpretation, a spiritual realization of man's history and destiny, in the light of the divine optimism and the promise of Israel's Prophets, will free us from the mastery, the tyranny, of fear and the clogging apathy of cynicism, with their consequent bitterness and inhumanity and greed, will girdle us about with strength and resolution, and will lead us out of the gloomy shadows of despondency and doubt into the sunshine of greater human progress, human fellowship, and happiness. We must saturate our souls with the spirit of the seers of Israel, whose inspiration sustained the great founders of this country and whose ideals mark every great forward movement of humankind. We must once more become imbued with their passion for humanity, for peace and social justice, their insistence that faith, righteousness and spiritual harmony, the groundwork of lasting human welfare, must supersede the self-centered quest of material gain, the greed for power and possession.

My dear young friends, yours has been a unique training. Here at Yeshiva College the reality of the spiritual life and experience has been the integrating principle in your education. Ideals of intellectual integrity and spiritual aspiration have been inculcated by a faculty of sound, creative scholarship and inspiring personality, in an environment where the distractions of extraneous urges could make little gain. You have been given scope to learn, that worth-while knowledge, as all genuine achievement, can be arrived at only by intellectual industry and honesty, open-mindedness, perseverance, and sympathetic understanding. You have been led to see that education, which is a continuous, a never-ceasing process, is more than the acquisition of factual information, the accumulation of however significant data and details. The goal of true education is power and love of thought, the ability to envisage life as a great unity, in a binding frame of intellectual and moral truth, and the devotion and consecration of learning to the steadfast service of mankind.

Complementing and deepening your general work, of high scholastic order, you have earnestly engaged in the study of the Bible, the source and fountain of spiritual knowledge and understanding, the God-given charter of spiritual life to mankind, as well as the Halacha and the Agada, the well springs of Jewish reason and Jewish vision. The Bible is the cornerstone upon which the founders and fathers of this great democracy reared the high structure of our national ideals. The spiritual strain of the seers of Israel, has been the golden thread in the continuous fabric of human unfoldment to our day, marking in human history the pattern of progress, often crowded by dark or bloody threads, but ever gleaming with the glorious faith and promise of human betterment. For the Bible is the source of living faith and the light of human love, and loyalty, to which nations as well as men must turn under the urge of the Divine Imperative.

You are going forth into a world that will probably offer no immediate opportunity to you all. We are still groping in the dark, however some may sense the approaching dawn. If there is soon to come the new day for which the heart of mankind yearns, it must be marked, not merely by the rising sun of material well-being, but by the golden dawn of a reviving faith, a reaffirmation of trust in G-d and faith in humanity, a faith that comforts, heals, strengthens, leads onward and forward, to a life of higher meaning, a destiny of greater spiritual enfoldment—in humble partnership with the Almighty—an illumination of the Infinitude within us, to a life spiritually aspiring and culturally creative.

Never has the world been in greater need of moving faith in its ultimate destiny. Fear and distrust, and the sown seeds of many conflicts are spread wide over the world; only by such faith can we purge ourselves of the inequities and iniquities of the passing ages. On such a faith, directed by such ideals, in the spirit of the eternal teachings of the Torah, rests the future of mankind.

It is our hope, it is our prayer, that you, my dear young friends, may ever be among the guardians of the ideals of mankind, that your life and your work may ever tend toward a more discerning restitution of the too often lost, the true and ultimate values of life, Israel's spiritual and moral truth, and inner happiness; that your faith in humanity's great future will hasten the dawning foreseen by the seers of Israel, the day of a new heart —the day when minds and hearts will work in harmony, when the mighty shall be girded with justice, when all children of men shall be as one brotherhood of humankind beneath the fatherhood of G-d, with faith and love directing the counsels of all lands, all persons and peoples inspirited by the profound and intimate pulsings of a new heart.

DR. SAFER'S MESSAGE

From a thousand colleges, within a month, some fifty thousand graduates will be sent forth, to swell the now slowly diminishing army of the unemployed. Their problem will not be, in any essential respect, different from that of the millions already seeking work; except that, instead of experience, they can exhibit only a sheepskin which proclaims them bachelors of art or bachelors of science. They soon find that preference is given to married men, particularly to those who for some years have been devoted to their work, and have become expert in their fields of life endeavor. The college graduate, in other words, is handicapped in competition with the young man of equal age who has had four years not of study, but of business. Unless he is planning to enter a professional field, for which college study is prerequisite, the graduate, looking around at the world today, may well question what good his degree has brought him.

The value of a college education is something that must be questioned, indeed, not only by the student and the graduate, but by all those concerned with the general well-being of the community, especially in a metropolis like New York City, which maintains three free colleges for its generations of growing citizens, and wherein are almost twenty other educational institutions of collegiate and university rank, including two that are among the largest in the world. However immediately practical the college graduate, hunting for a job, may be in his estimate of the worth of the four years he has spent in absorbing the subjects and amassing the points required for his degree, the community may perhaps be forgiven if it looks with less interested eye on the graduate's pocketbook, and turns its attention upon other aspects and values of his college education. In the minds of many, too many even of the students themselves, the function of the college of liberal arts and science has been confused with that of the technical and the professional schools. These institutions, it is obvious and true, are designed to equip their students with the training necessary for carrying on, in later life, a specific type of activity: —engineering, teaching, medicine, the law. They are, for maturer years, the equivalent of the trade school and the technical high school. they are the modern counterpart of apprenticeship and "reading" for a profession. The college of liberal arts and science has quite another function, holds quite another position, another significance, in the scheme of higher education. Its aim is to lead its students, not to do something, but to be something. Not specific training, but character and culture, are its goal.

The leaders of our land, of all lands, are drawn increasingly from the ranks of the college graduates. Whether, indeed, they rise to individual prominence or remain undistinguished among their communities, it is ultimately from them that the cultural ideals of the land must emanate, from them that the leaven must come to lift the level of intelligence, of tolerance, of liberal and truly democratic acceptance of the many racial traditions and cultural and ethical systems that meet in this land, to combine and to fuse them into the high American spirit and truly American ideals. Especially in these days, when the darkness of medieval intolerance and "racial" persecution has engulfed a great European nation, it is essential to keep in mind the spiritual and cultural aspects of college life, and to find in them the true significance of the years spent in a college of liberal arts and after these the years given to the community. For every life, no matter how spent, is given to the community, is a living model for good or for ill; and his years at college become to the thoughtful graduate a responsibility and a pledge to something more than a spree at football reunions, to a maintenance of the long tradition of spirituality and culture of which he has briefly partaken, but by which, we trust, he has been permanently inspired.

It is in this connection that my thoughts turn to Yeshiva College, of which I am proud to be the Dean. Situated on Washington Heights, Manhattan's highest point, Yeshiva College is in a sense a symbol of the heights of liberalism and tolerance our country has achieved, for it was founded, six years ago, by the very people that through the years have been subject to persecution and repression and are at this moment in Germany feeling the oppressor's hand. The only college of liberal arts and sciences in America under Jewish auspices, though it accepts all qualified students and its faculty consists of scholars, Jews and non-Jews alike—Yeshiva College is devoted to the creation of an atmosphere where the age-old verities and the fruits of modern knowledge may be coordinated and compatibly absorbed. The significance of this direct entry of American Jewry—long recognized by patrons and seekers of learning—in the field of higher education has been widely acclaimed, and at the coming commencement, the Hon. Herbert H. Lehman, Governor of New York State, will address the graduates. Yet the ideal of Yeshiva College is but an expression from the Jewish point of view of the ideal of all the liberal arts colleges, of all schools of liberal arts and science in the great universities. It is natural that most of these institutions were denominational in origin, for they rose out of a concern, not for the individual's livelihood, but for the well-being of the community, which I need not emphasize, depends upon the state of being of the men and women who are its citizens.

The times are out of joint. Individuals in high places, here and abroad, have bemired our trust that the common decencies of life, that honesty, tolerance, magnanimity, understanding—in short, that spirituality and culture, will dominate and direct our lives. It is for their fostering of the ideals inherent in these aspects of life, for their *disinterested* pursuit of knowledge and development of character, that we turn to the liberal arts colleges, and hope that in their spirit, and bearing their ideals, will rise the country's leaders of tomorrow.

CONFIDENCE
To Franklin D. Roosevelt

Through all the darkness that enshrouds Today
   And leaves behind its poison of despair,
Through hopelessness, an unexpected ray
   Foreshows the utter banishment of care.
An unforeshadowed ray, a tiny hope,
   More glorious than a nabob's opulence,
Enlivens man, who need no longer grope
   Since he is fortified by Confidence.

What peerless giant, what colossal force
   Has suddenly performed this miracle?
To what great instrument had he recourse
   To help him do the unbelievable?
A single word to those who seemed forlorn
   And with it hope and confidence were born.

—BERNARD DOV MILIANS

THE TRAGEDY OF GERMANY

History is replete with the shattered illusions of mankind. Monuments of majestic splendor have been conjured up out of the fertility of the human mind to bask in the warm rays of specious reality and then fade into the ephemeral realm of lost dreams. The most recent of these fallen idols is the much-vaunted epitome of human progress— Deutsche Kultur. A Hegel might, with self-righteous ingenuity, place Teutonic civilization as the synthesis of all human effort, but we, of this day and age, may, with even more righteous indignation, assign to a civilization productive of a Hitler the ignominious position of antithesis to all that is noble and worthwhile in the lofty aspirations of civilized man.

Persecution of the Jew is not a new nor an unusual phenomenon. It has been the peculiar fate of the Jew to receive the scorpion-like stings of Fate in far greater measure than any other race. The sharp crack of the whip and the corporal scourge of fire and sword are more the rule than the exception in Jewish history. Why, then, has the conscience of civilized man been aroused to so sudden a pitch of universal condemnation by the recent atrocities perpetrated by the present German government?

We of the present generation have regarded, with increasing interest and hope, the efforts of those altruistic souls whose lives have been devoted to the stamping out of intolerance and the maintenance of world peace. We have seen a League of Nations flower from the blood-drenched fields of the late war. We have heard denunciations of intolerance and discrimination voiced from the pulpits of all denominations, from the convention halls of all sorts of organizations, from the public fora of every land. Barbarism had been, but was no more.

The dream has ended, as all dreams do. And in its wake has come disillusionment. Germany has betrayed the hopes of mankind. Political, economic, and social isolation would have been a blow sufficiently devastating of the lives of the six hundred thousand Jews in Germany. But Germany's return to medieval barbarism stamps her culture as a sham, her refinement as camouflage, and her sense of right and wrong as so horribly perverted that the tortures of a Torquemada were tolerated in twentieth-century Berlin. Would that those Jews were alive, who so confidently and arrogantly proclaimed that from Germany goes forth the Torah and the word of the Lord from Berlin.

Once again we are brought face to face with the inevitable reality. Poultices and compresses are mere temporary balsam to the harassed and lacerated body of the Jew. One road of promise is open—the road to Palestine, the national Jewish homeland.

THE NEED FOR AN ENDOWMENT

Life beckons to another flock of college graduates. Though its welcoming gestures seem rather weary and mechanical, still youth needs no second invitation. Depressions may come and go, but the search for knowledge goes on forever. At a time when all about us the effects of economic stress have rendered thousands homeless and hungry, it seems almost a crime to divert funds for much-needed aid into the channels of education. Universities and colleges all over the country have felt this attitude manifested in the tremendous decline of their income for running expenses. Yeshiva College has been no exception.

The physical well-being of man is an essential component of progress. The advance of civilization has been marked by the gradual improvement of the living conditions of mankind. But always there has been recognized the underlying substratum of progress, the spiritual and intellectual development of the human mind. To this purpose the colleges of all ages have been dedicated; and there has been no finer investment for the family of men than the continued support of these centres of learning. A college progresses and expands in proportion to the facility with which it can meet its financial obligations. Thus, colleges of to-day live and grow on their endowments. Any college, which must resort to a "hand to mouth" policy for its support, must ultimately fail. By failure, I mean failure both in the necessary offices of careful supervision of a student's work and activities, failure in the disgruntled attitude of teachers who have not been compensated for their work, and failure in so far as the students themselves are affected by

the precarious basis upon which their alma mater rests. In our own institution we have not yet reached so grave a pass. Our teachers are still enthusiastic, our students optimistic, and our administration actively interested in the individual work of each student. But "an ounce of prevention is worth a pound of cure" and credit should be given to those far-sighted men who have so zealously advocated the establishment of an endowment fund for the support of Yeshiva College. An endowment would not only insure the permanence of an institution upon whose maintenance depends the future of Judaism in this country, but it would offer the basis for that necessary expansion and growth which would make of Yeshiva College what it should be and what we hope it will be—one of the great universities of the world.

A beginning has already been made and several men have given liberally of their time and money for the development of this project. There has been organized the Yeshiva Endowment Fund, Inc., whose purpose is to interest men in patronizing Yeshiva College, as well to supervise the investment of the money that has already been contributed. Every effort should be bent in this direction. Therein lies *salvation;* therein lies *expansion;* therein lies the future of *Judaism* in America.

Prometheus Or Tantalus?

By

ERNEST RAPHAEL

Shall man's hopes repose softly upon saffron cushions of a blissful Heaven, or shall they toss feverishly upon the hard bed of an implacable Nature? Is man a child of the gods, or a chance wanderling in lonely space? Is consciousness, as the idealist contends, the architect of the universe, or merely a throbbing impulse in a world of atomic disturbances? In a word, is man a Prometheus in possession of divine secrets, or a Tantalus condemned forever to reach but never to grasp?

The medieval age—that dismal chasm where sophistry and error lay in fond embrace—evolved a most ingenious solution to these perplexing problems. Man was the noblest of all creations. His life was a mortal conflict between good and evil, a conflict that terminated in eternal bliss or eternal damnation. In the vaulted heaven, man read the glory of an omnipotent G-d, and in the sulphurous gases escaping from the yawning jaws of volcanic mountains he fancied the faint traces of Purgatory. The earth on which he lived was but an island suspended in space, midway between a glorious heaven and a torturous hell.

In the sixteenth century, the investigations of Galileo, Copernicus, and Kepler threatened man's monarchical pretensions, and shook the medieval structure to its very foundation. Man fought against his dethronement with the ferocity of an animal at bay, and in G-d's name he persecuted Galileo and burned Giordano Bruno at the stake. But with the triumph of reason, man was compelled to give up the medieval Paradise woven out of the tenuous threads of dialectic, together with the multi-shaped mirrors of phantasy in which man had often surveyed his exaggerated beauty and importance. A universe of law and order succeeded a universe ruled by divine petulance and discrimination. A materialistc perspective was introduced into the investigations of Nature, a per-spective that received its most eulogistic, though declamatory, expression in the work of Holbach.

For the preservation of man's privileged position in the universe there were two avenues of escape. The first, suggested by Pomponazzi, urged the sharp distinction between reason and religion. Reason, and its handmaid philosophy, became concerned with logical investigations in the secular realm, while religion with its theological doctrines was placed beyond the pale of proof into the realm of belief. For reason to seek theologic consecration was abusrd; for theology to offer rational proof for its propositions was fantastic. Thus Pomponazzi declared immortality of the soul to be logically insoluble, but solemnly affirmed it as an article of faith. Logically, it may be observed in passing, this approach was a return to the Tertullian doctrine, *Credo quia absurdum;* and historically it marked the breakdown of scholastism, viz., the effort to establish the rational nature of theological propositions.

The second avenue of escape, as observed in the writings of Boehme, involved the sharp dualism of the visible and the invisible worlds. Beneath the surface of visible things there is concealed a deep mystery, which is unravelled by the soul through mystical revelation. Though Boehme reaffirmed many of the propositions of theology, we cannot fail to catch glimpses of his liberation from the vagaries of mediaeval scholasticism. Science cannot, according to Boehme, dislodge religion from its venerable position. On the contrary, the divine Spirit dwells in the body of nature, as the soul dwells in the body of man. But any cosmological dualism, as Paulsen has pointed out, when carried to its logical conclusion reduces itself to monism or at best to pantheism, and consequently we need not be surprised to find Boehme occasionally equating God and nature. The pantheisim, feebly and confusedly suggested by Boehme, was developed independently by Bruno, and by Spinoza in whom the material and spiritual, temporal and eternal, find the most eloquent union.

The anthropocentric aspects of philosophical speculation, however, received their death-blow at the hands of enlightened propagandists and journalists—the French "philosophes" of the eighteenth century. The most characteristic feature of eighteenth-century French rationalism was the social transvaluation which it gave to all metaphysical speculation. Thus Berkeley's arguments in his *New Theory of Vision* to the effect that the shape and size of objects are not given in immediate sensation but are intellectual constructions were used by Diderot to establish the relativity of morals and political institutions. Locke's empirical psychology was urged by the "philosophes" as a basis for universal education. All abstract speculation was given by these enlightened thinkers a social transformation. The "philosophes" were not metaphysicians. First and last, they were reformers.

The first extension of reason was into the realm of politics and social reform. Voltaire, influenced by Newton's mathematical procedure, contended that reason must be adopted as an instrument of reform. Reason had produced law and order in the cosmos; and reason must produce law and order in society. So strong was his faith in reason that he believed that all the profound and innumerable forces which chained man to an irrational past could be dissolved by the single touch of the magic wand of reason. At first glance this notion seems highly superficial, but it contained the kernel of a great truth—the notion of progress. Man was no longer to dream, amid squalor and misery, of a golden past, but was to apply his own efforts for the amelioration of his sufferings. Man, endowed with reason, was to effect the ultimate regeneration of the society in which he lived. The natural man was glorified by Voltaire not out of a romantic weakness, but because he served as a convenient symbol, as a physical representation of man free from the institutional evils perpetuated in society by kingly avarice and priestly knavery.

Reason then invaded the sphere of morals and found its expression in Helvetius' *L'Esprit*. An inveterate foe of mysticism and asceticism, Helvetius brought a new theory of morals and human character. All human virtue, said Helvetius in effect, was motivated by self-love. Man sought good and shunned evil because it brought him pleasure and spared him pain. To speak of a thing as good in itself was to utter nonsense. How Helvetius deduced social responsibility from the principle of self-interest is beyond the scope of this essay. Suffice it to realize that Helvetius rejected the divine ordinances of the church and the mad ravings of the mystics in preference for experience pure and simple as the basis for moral action.

The final extension of reason was made by Holbach in his *System of Nature*. Few books have made such an impression on mankind as this one. It seemed to many that they stood face to face with the devil, come to claim their souls. The universe, they read in the eloquent pages of Holbach, was nothing but matter in motion; G-d was at best the personification of a force, cold and inanimate; the existence of a soul was chimerical; the belief in man's eternity was a vain flattery that must be eradicated if he is to attain happiness in this world. Man, believed to be a fondling of the gods, was but a fleeting symmetry in a world of atomic interaction. The terror that such assertions produced must have been enormous. As Goethe said of the book; "it came to us so grey, so Cimmerian, so corpselike, that we could not endure its pressure; we shuddered before it, as if it had been a spectre. It struck us as the very quintessence of musty age, savourless, repugnant." Caught in the stream of Holbach's eloquence, man suddenly discovered himself an inhabitant, as it were, of a huge strange city. He had been awakened from a delightful dream only to find himself in the clutches of omnipotent Death. A terror seized him and he fled to romanticism, in which he rediscovered spirit, heaven, purpose, harmony and fantasy. Rousseau clearly indicates to us the psychologic origins of his romanticism in the follow-

(*Continued on Page* 58)

Shakespeare—
"To Be Or Not To Be"

By

ABRAHAM S. GUTERMAN

In the past fifty years there has been growing up a considerable movement among literary detectives to prove by various means that Shakespeare did not write the works accredited to him. The reader will be justified in asking what difference it makes who really wrote these works. We have them and we enjoy them. They adorn our national literature and are permanent models of power, beauty, and eloquence in the realm of expression.

In response to this query, I shall endeavor to justify the seemingly idle Shakespearian research in this direction. With the birth of man, came the birth of curiosity. From the moment that earth's first picture unfolded itself before man's wondering gaze, he was filled with the mystery of things. The effort to pierce this veil and fathom hidden secrets is the foundation stone of all progress. To it belong the advance and self-improvement of mankind through the ages. To it belong the glories of our present civilization and upon it will depend the world that is to be.

Men of the past were at times negligent of their duty to posterity. They failed to register their finds, to record the events of their centuries, to explain the ideals which they prized. At times they shouted down the protagonist of a new discovery, and at times they dispensed with an obnoxious representative of progress by recourse to fire and sword.

History of every kind, literary, political, social, and economic, has thus suffered tremendously by the shortsightedness of men. Events, movements, migrations, masterpieces of poetry and of art, all these must now be unearthed to tell the story of past civilizations, and many of these archaic discoveries must be supplemented by the profuse use of our imaginations. But strive we must and strive we shall to uncover the mystery of the past so that we may build more certainly for the elusive future.

We thus feel that every effort designed to ascertain accurately a historic fact is another step in the advance of progress. If, at every step in the development of science, we had asked whither and what use, all advance would have been stifled. The past holds out a challenge to us. Pragmatically it aids humankind but little to determine exactly when some specific event hidden in antiquity took place. But the sum total of human knowledge is just as much a part of man's conquest of the earth as is his desire for present comfort and pleasure. It is thus of historical interest to know exactly who really is the author of "Shakespeare's" works.

Then, too, there is much that this information could contribute to the psychology of genius. If the Shakespeare who is described in our biographies is the author, then a study of his early environment, the milieu in which his plays were written, his early training, his family life, all these can shed much light on a rapidly growing subject of investigation. If, on the other hand, someone else wrote the plays, the same points in this unknown's life would assist us to understand by what high pathway one genius entered so gloriously into the Arcadian sanctuary of the Muse. We might learn whether entrance to her Arcadian garden is gained by wide and deep scholarship, by sudden inspiration, or whether she bestows her graces upon the votaries who fortuitously receive the designation of her wand.

There is still another important reason for ascertaining the actual author of these works. It is a well-known fact that we can never separate an author entirely from the works that he has written.

If it can be proven conclusively that someone other than Shakespeare created the works, we may, by studying this unknown's life and thought, understand more thoroughly many of the plays, see some of them perhaps as autobiographical, trace perhaps in their development some genius of multiple personality, who can combine the pensiveness of a Hamlet, the jealousy of an Othello, and the ruthless ambition of a Macbeth. The works may then have, for us, a new interest and, if it were possible, a greater.

The first point that strikes us in the pursuit of this study is the mystery that shrouds Shakespeare's life. Few of the facts of his career have been adequately substantiated. And if we accept the descriptions presented to us, we are thereby stirred to question whether the man whom the biographies depict could have written on so high a literary plane.

Thus, the arguments against the Shakespearian authorship presented by the so-called Anti-Stratfordians resolve themselves into two divisions—the mysteries and the improbabilities. The first mystery, besides the uncertainty concerning the facts of Shakespeare's life in general, is the fact that his death was passed by completely unnoticed by his contemporaries. When Spenser and Beaumont died, a chorus of lamentations, of poetic appreciations swept through England. When Ben Jonson died in 1637, forty poets wrote expressions of their grief, and their verse occupied 64 pages of a complete edition of his work. When Shakespeare died in 1616, strangely enough no poet was stirred to record his passing in verse, and even Ben Jonson remained silent. Is there not a tone of strangeness in "Sweetest Shakespeare, Fancy's Child," who for years had been producing poetry of matchless beauty, being thus unnoticedly lowered into his grave? Mystery the first!

Then, in 1623, when the immortal bard's work was for the first time issued in a complete edition, the same Ben Jonson designated him as "not of an age but of all time." A rather belated tribute! What cause could Jonson have had for withholding his adulatory verses for so many years? Mystery the second!

Again, the folio of 1623 contains a portrait of Shakespeare engraved by Martin Droeshut. A careful study of the head of this figure, of its rigidity and strange stiffness, shows it to be a mask. An examination of the sleeves of the coat show that the front half and back half of a left arm are also superimposed on the picture. Why these peculiar additions? Can they be mere coincidences? Or were they meant to represent the fact that under the mask of Shakespeare some other author has been writing with his left hand; for one attributes to the left hand symbolically those acts which the right hand cannot acknowledge. Mystery, the third!

In 1790, the diary of Philip Henslowe, the great Elizabethan producer, was discovered. It contained the authors and actors of his time, the plays he bought, and the amount he paid for each. Shakespeare is not even mentioned in this document, and it is hardly possible that Henslowe would have been unacquainted with the greatest playwright of the time. This leads to the question, was the Shakespeare we know the greatest playwright of his time? Mystery the fourth!

We now turn to the realm of the improbabilities. It is here that the anti-Stratfordians direct their most powerful broadsides. Picture a man born of illiterate parents, whose schooling was of the most meagre. He deserts his wife, and becomes an actor in London. He writes purely for money and breaks off suddenly, returning to provincial life as if dissociating entirely his art from himself. He dies without being in the possession of a single book. Now consider a monument of works that proclaim their author to be a classical scholar, a diplomat, soldier, lawyer, sportsman, musician, doctor, botanist, naturalist, falconer, sailor, astronomer, even an archer and an angler. Conceive a vocabulary employed that surpasses the most extensive vocabularies in all languages. Thackeray's vocabulary was about 5000; Milton's, next to Shakespeare's greatest among English writers, was about 7000. Victor Hugo, with the most extensive vocabulary in the French language, had but 9000 words. The estimates of Shakespeare's vocabulary go from 15,000 to 24,000 words.

Is there any wonder that doubt should enter a thoughtful mind that this versatile genius, master of so wide a range of human knowledge, should be this ordinary man? Moreover, argue the unorthodox, this same almost omniscient individual could barely scrawl an illegible, illiterate signature, besides not knowing the spelling of his own name. This formidable array of evidence must cause us to pause and give ear. Can grapes grow on thorns?

We have presented up to this point the general outline of the Anti-Stratfordian attack. Let us now consider the validity of some of its contentions. The almost complete silence about Shakespeare by his contemporaries should not cause us any undue concern. We are dealing with the 16th and not with the 20th century. I daresay that theatregoers of to-day rarely take the trouble to find out who the author of the play presented is, with the exception, of course, of certain popularly known dramatists. We know but a few dates of birth, death, entrance at school, college, and Inns of the Court, of many of Shakespeare's illustrious contemporaries. In this period, the characters and personalities of mere playwrights were not closely followed. Only such men were generally known as gained popularity by occupying public position, like Spenser, or by being active in court society, like Sydney; or those who gained notoriety by writing about feuds and friendships, like Greene and Nash, by writing reminiscences and satires, like Ben Jonson, by killing anyone, like Ben Jonson, by being killed, like Marlowe, or by being imprisoned with the danger of having nose and ears split, like Marston. The age was not very enthusiastic about mere dramatists. Thus silence obscures the life and personality of Kyd, Beaumont, Fletcher, Dekker and others. Nor need we concede that the author of Shakespeare must have been a scholar of the first order. We find many instances in the works which point to a rather cursory acquaintance in the field of scholarship. In "Troilus and Cressida" the Greeks and Trojans cite Aristotle—a rather unscholarly anachronism. In "The Winter's Tale" he calls Delphi

Delphos, confusing Delphos with Delos, thus placing the Delphic oracle on an island. In the same play he makes the artist Giulio Romano (1492-1546) contemporary with the oracle of the Pythian Apollo. Is it likely that a scholar would place guns in Scotland three hundred years before the invention of artillery, or represent Cleopatra finding diversion in the comparatively modern game of billiards?

How, ask the anti-Stratfordians, could the son of such illiterate parents with so little training have written these plays? History furnishes us with countless examples of men of lowly birth rising to the highest pinnacles of genius. Thus, Giotto was a shepherd boy; Leonardo da Vinci, the illegitimate son of a common notary; Wolsey's father was a butcher; Marlowe worked as a shoemaker and Ben Jonson as a bricklayer; Burns was the son of a small farmer, and Keats was an apothecary's apprentice.

A man who could hardly spell his own name, they insist, could not have indited such immortal verse. It is true that the signatures left to us of Shakespeare are spelt in different ways, but the spelling of surnames at the time was even more inconsistent than the spelling of ordinary words. For example, Sir Walter Raleigh is known to have spelt his name in five different ways, viz., Rawley, Raleghe, Ralegh, Rawleigh, and Rawleghe. Thus, the variation in spelling has no special significance. And as to the illegibility of the handwriting, it is a fault to which many of us may with perfect candor plead guilty.

But, even if we grant that Shakespeare is not the author of the works that bear his name, who is? The Anti-Stratfordians are divided into many camps. For one, Bacon is Shakespeare. For another, Rutland is Shakespeare. For yet another Derby is Shakespeare, and for still another Oxford is Shakespeare. One group modifies the Baconian theory by designating Bacon, not as the individual author of the works, but as the editor and supervisor of a group of the eminent young dramatists of the time, who in collaboration wrote the plays. And another group designates the author as the

"Great Unknown" who is yet to be discovered.

Let us turn then to examine the evidence and weigh the arguments presented by some of these groups. We shall start with the Baconians, for they have gone farthest in the development of their thesis. Many distinguished men have taken up this theory, including Emerson, Gervinus, Disraeli, Hawthorne, Lowell, O. W. Holmes and Dickens.

No other figure of the Elizabethan period combined so egregiously the various fields of learning manifested in the " 'Shakespeare' Works". He was all that the works required their writer to be. He was both philosopher and poet. Thus claim the Baconians.

They base their contentions on three essential points. In the first place, a careful study of both authors shows that their minds coincide, that their geographical knowledge, political ideas and religions sentiments were similar. Secondly, the many parallelisms between their works, the employment of similar expressions, quotations and errors indicates the same mind operating in both cases. Thirdly, there appear to be hidden in the "Shakespeare" works all sort of anagrams, cryptograms, and other concealed forms of expression which point to Francis Bacon, Lord Verulam, Viscount St. Alban, Lord Chancellor of England as the writer of the "works."

As to the similarity in ideas and expression between Bacon and Shakespeare, we may remain unconvinced of their identity. Two men of high and noble mind, living in the same generation, imbibing the spirit and knowledge of their time, would inevitably show a certain similarity in their ideas and even, when discussing the same subject, a great similarity in the expression of those ideas. The hundreds of parallelisms which scholars have drawn up to prove this theory would have little validity if we remember that treatment of any given subject by two gifted men, trained in the concepts of the age, would have a certain likeness in approach, in choice of examples, and often in choice of language.

The phase of proof that deals with the concealed testimony of Bacon's authorship, written into the

works, is the most startling, the most interesting and the most precarious. From earliest times, hidden forms of expression, known only to initiates who had gained in some way the esoteric keys, were both a favorite pastime and a necessary vehicle for conveying information. Mystics from time immemorial have delighted in searching the Scriptures for hidden information of this sort. Sects have been founded whose secrets were recorded in well-ordered codes. The source of many of these codes has been the Cabala with its Gematria, or simple clock count, w h e r e A=1, B=2, C=3, etc., or the reverse count, where Z=1, Y=2, X=3, or the Kay count, where K=10, L=11, etc. All these various methods were a part of the mystical literature for centuries before the Elizabethan Era.

By a study of the records and writings of the Rosicrucian society, or the society of the Rose Cross,—Rose representing secrecy, and Cross representing salvation of humankind,—which flowered during the Elizabethan period, we find that Bacon was one of its prominent members, that it aimed at the advancement of human knowledge, that it employed the above-mentioned methods of concealed expression to keep its secrets sácred for the "Sons of Sapience." Thus, we may be reasonably sure that Bacon was acquainted with the inweaving of special messages into the warp and woof of literary productions. Moreover, Bacon had declared, in the works we do credit to him, that advancement of humankind could be best effected by romance and poetry. This would explain the great moral lessons of the Shakespearian dramas.

Let us pause to regard some instances of this hidden type of expression. Though there have been brought forward all sorts of cryptograms, anagrams, and cabalistic arrangements proving Bacon to be the author, we shall glance at but a few.

In "Love's Labour's Lost" Act V, Sc. I, we encounter the peculiar word, Honorificabilitudinitatibus. This word seems to cry for some explanation. The Baconians come to the rescue and declare it to be an anagram which, when rearranged, contains the Latin sentence . . . Hi ludi tuiti sibi Fr. Bacono nati (These plays, entrusted to themselves, proceeded from Francis Bacon). Now, a different form of the same word is found on a private document of Bacon. There the word is "honorificabilitudino" which, they say, is the anagram for . . . Initio hi ludi Fr. Bacono. (In the beginning these plays are from Francis Bacon). These anagrams have a strangely coincidental persistence, and it is little wonder that numbers of people stake their reputation in defence of this theory.

On page 53 of the Shakespeare Folio Comedies, the name Bacon is introduced. And to render the Bacon-Shakespeare secret apparent, the number of words on page 53 is exactly 177 which is the simple clock or Cabbala count for *William Shakespeare*. The word "honorificabilitudinitatibus", referred to above, is by simple clock count 287, which is in turn the sum of *F. Bacon-W. Shakespeare* by the Reverse Count. The sum of *Fra Rosierosse*, the designation of the Rosicrucian Brotherhood, is 157 by the simple clock count. The sum of *Bacon-W. Shakespeare* is also 157 by the same count and the same number of letters is found in the garbled inscription from the Tempest on the Shakespeare monument in Westminster Abbey.

In my opinion, there is no more effective refutation of this sort of manipulation of figures and letters than the cryptogram of S. James of Leeds who, by proper arrangement of the titles of several of the plays, proves that Bernard Shaw wrote Shakespeare.

Mac .... *Beth*
Oth .... *Ello*
Comedy of Er*R*ors
Merch of Ve*N*ice
Coriol .... *A*nus
Mids Night D*R*eam
Merry Wiv. of *D*sor
Meas. for Mea*S*ure
Much Adoab N*H*ing
Anth. and Cl. *A*tra
All's well .... *W*ell

This *reductio ad absurdum* should give pause to our credence in acrostics, anagrams, or imagined ciphers.

One of the caustic critics of this theory has said, "The idea of robbing the world of Shakespeare for such a stiff legal-headed old jackass as Bacon is a modern invention of fools."

Any reasonable person would object to the violence of this denunciation. It is unfair to the scholars who have devoted years of their life in producing evidence in support of this theory. But belief in their sincerity should in no way restrain us from rigorous criticism as to the validity of their arguments. Defamation proves nothing. Reason may convince even avowed anti-Stratfordians.

It would be beyond the scope of this discussion to present in detail the other theories of the Shakespearian authorship. They are built largely on surmise, and the few proofs discovered to support their contention are of a shadowy nature. The Rutland theory depends mainly on the connection between Rutland's report of his embassy to Denmark in 1603, and the references to Danish habits and customs in the 1604 Quarto of Hamlet. Since Shakespeare may have read the report or spoken to Rutland, the weight of this argument is negligible. Two other gentlemen, the sixth Earl of Derby and the seventeenth Earl of Oxford, have been offered as candidates for this enviable post. The evidence in support of these latter two is as limited as that of the Rutland theory. And we feel impelled to conclude that the "Great Unknown", proposed by some critics as the author of the works, despite all the theories, might just as well have been William Shakespeare.

In the field of literature, the mysteries are legion. Did a sightless bard chant thousands of years ago the story of the siege of Troy, and was that bard Homer? Or is he the innocent bearer of a fame that belongs to many? Were the gossamers of struggle and triumph and defeat that we know as the epic cycles of the Middle Ages the product of single geniuses, or are they merely the collections of the labors of a group? Did an Ossian

(Continued on page 53)

Aspects of Judaism

By
RABBI DR. LEO JUNG

I.

SOME ASPECTS OF JUDAISM

Judaism is the religion of the Jew. It is based on the Torah of Moses. Torah means direction. We look upon the Torah as the direction to happy and noble life.

The faith in the revelation of God's Will is the immovable foundation of Jewish survival. Without acceptance of the authority of the Torah, a Jewish generation, however brilliant, powerful, philanthropic, has in the many instances of our historical experience proved too weak to withstand the assaults of outside influences. With the elimination of that faith, the Jewish community had eliminated its vital force, and rapidly disappeared in the majority.

Beyond this principle Judaism has no dogma. From time to time problems have arisen, the formulation of which, or the solution to which, seemed to touch foundations of the faith, and during certain of these periods Judaism's attitude toward these ideas was considered as of dogmatic importance. But their importance shrunk as new problems began to focus general attention on themselves.

Judaism knows no literalism or fundamentalism. The text of the Bible is subjected to ever new interpretations, and each new interpretation has been hailed as the fruit of the faith, and welcomed as an additional source of mental and spiritual enrichment. This principle is not a child of our liberal age, but has been acted upon for the last two millennia, by rabbi and learned layman alike.

II.

THE METHOD OF JUDAISM

For Jewish life, however, this interpreting activity, whilst fruitful and encouraging, is not all-important. When a Jewish boy reaches religious maturity (at the age of thirteen), he is not asked or admonished as to faith and interpretation, he is enjoined as to the traditional ideals and observances

of Jewish life. In Jewish thought the division has long been recognized between obvious social postulates like honesty, chastity, love of one's neighbor, and between what are called ceremonies. This division, however, was not made in the Bible. The Torah embraces every aspect of life and its text knows of no division between "ceremonial" and moral law. In Judaism they are co-ordinated. Judaism has demanded from its adherents loyalty to its social ideals. But Judaism has never been satisfied with the mere call to great ideals. Humanity, according to the Torah, needs more than announcements, however solemn or emphatic, of abstract goals. General great ideals have a habit of impressing our emotions without influencing our conduct. Judaism holds that a training is necessary in a habit which will always consider the ideal, that the ideal must be brought home, first by humanitarian exercises, then by symbols and ceremonies, conveying emotional experiences which keep the vision of beauty and goodness before the people, without which view the ideal becomes stale, a futile phrase.

Thus "Love thy neighbor as thyself" is twice enjoined in Leviticus, the third book of the Torah of Moses. But the very same chapter insists on the practical realization of its implication. It demands part of our annual harvest as our minimum contribution to our poor neighbor. The ceremonial of Jewish holidays is a veritable symphony of goodness, from the gift to the poor on the eve of the holy day "so that the stranger at our gate too, may rejoice on the day of our feast," to the many religious acts and symbols expressive of cosmopolitan human sympathy.

The ceremony indeed is the *method* of Judaism. It connects practical life in all its variety and all its activities with the spiritual truths of religion; it gives tangible form to those ideas and ideals. Judaism not only states the ideal, but consistently,

in every instance, provides the method and outlines the path, toward its realization. This is another aspect of the comparative mistrust the Torah
has for mere theoretical speculation unrelated to
conduct.

The Mitzvah or ceremony speaks both *to* the
Jew and *for* him. By insisting on certain actions
and prayers in moments of great emotional dis-
turbance, the ceremony reduces the expenditure of
emotional energy and steadies our heartbeat, pre-
venting us from losing balance, in hours, alike, of
extreme happiness or unhappiness.

III.
THE WORKMANSHIP OF JUDAISM

The ceremony speaks to us, pointing out spiritual
vistas to encourage our moral effort; the ceremony
speaks for us, articulating our sorrows and joys,
when expression, though vital; is impossible because
of pent-up feeling. The ceremony thus trains us
in self restraint and in constant vision of that good
and beauty which we are to achieve by our own
effort. Recognizing the need for occasional up-
lifting above the humdrum drabness of life, the
Torah through ceremony, diverts our gaze above
the sphere of cut-throat competition, social annoy-
anecs and personal disabilities, toward a contem-
plation of a better world, of which we should not
merely dream but for the consummation of which
the ideal calls and the ceremony guides our steps.

The Torah stated the divine command "Love
thy neighbor as thyself." As a means towards
the realization of this precept, the Torah has the
principle of the foreigner's equality before the
Law; of the civic duty to help the poor, and to
take care of the stranger. Such activity, not dependent upon a man's temper, or mood, but representing the legal minimum of his contributions
to social welfare, is the first step towards the realization of that ideal. The obligation to take care
of non-Jewish poor as well as of the Jewish desti-
tute, tends to make these steps more valuable, to
train the Jew towards a general humanitarian tend-
ency. Our ceremonies, such the one described,
are the source of humanitarian vision, the springs
of kindliness which feed interdenominational friend-
ship and influence action.

IV.
G-D-CONSCIOUSNESS

But behind them all is the revelation that all
these things are not merely fine deeds, they derive
their importance from the fact that their performance
is the revealed will of G-d. To the Jew, the one
good in life is conformity with the will of G-d.
Sin is refusal to accept the law of G-d or action
against it.

The Jew, according to the Jewish Bible, is not
the *only* child of G-d, but his spiritual firstborn,
carrier of the Father's message. He is charged
with the message and to safeguard it; he must go
his own way, live his own life, protect the separate-
ness of his march thru history, protect the pristine
purity of his faith, protect the very uniqueness of
his destiny, resist every influence, that would change
his message, develop thru centuries his mode of
expression, the force of his example, the influence
of his heirloom, *the Torah*, so that his labor for
the ideal might be successful.

The *ultimate goal* is the penetration of every
nation with the living ideal of ethical monotheism
to a degree which will beautify life, unite man and
banish wickedness from the world.

The task is dependent on the capacity of Israel
to walk his way thru the ages, trained in G-d-
consciousness, isolated during the centuries of
struggles, in the world but not of it. The discipline
of suffering for the ideal, the discipline of struggle
for freedom of conscience, the *hard battle* against
passion, desire, vanity, they are to help the Jew
to retain his identity, and thru his identity the un-
diluted strength of his message, his G-d-consciousness as the single propelling force in his individual
and collective life. Hence every Jewish ceremony
is part of the G-d-given way of life, every com-
mandment based on the will of G-d, every step
prescribed by G-d, or nullified by its non-con-
formity with His will.

When the message underlying the Jewish ceremonies is appreciated these latter become the wings
by which the Jew lifts himself into the sphere of
his historical ideal, which help him to defeat the
downward pull of gravitation. But if they are
not related to the totality of Jewish life, they be-

come a leaden weight.

Ceremonies are the wheels of his progress towards social righteousness. But if thru ignorance, lassitude, indifference, their meaning is not known, they become clogs. Some Jews impatient with the slow progress of humanitarian effort, unaware of the fact that wheels need a driving spirit, discard the wheels, deny the value of ceremonies and then censure the vehicle for its inability to move forward.

We are a minority. A minority comes into being out of a consciousness of some immanent difference which distinguishes it from the majority. A minority can survive only as long as a consciousness of this difference and a recognition of its worthwhileness prevail in the minds of its members. It may be astonishing to friend and foe that we Jews are but one percent of humanity. It is a surpassingly hard task for a scattered minority of one percent to reach longevity. The struggle for national survival is accentuated by the levelling tendencies of the industrial age, by the rearousing of cosmopolitan hope and endeavor, by international, interracial, interdenominational class struggle. All these tendencies represent so many unceasing assaults on our personal Jewishness, on our national existence.

We have no refuge, no unassailable fortress other than the Jewish life, the atmosphere, in which the Lord is set continually before us. The laws of the Torah in their totality create the Jewish environment, in which the Jew works out his salvation for the salvation of man. Thru a number of customs, laws, regulations, admonitions, encouragements, cognitions the Jew is to be kept in contact with the divine spirit. No secular pursuits need interfere for one moment with this essential relationship, which is the true object of religion. On the contrary, by means of customs, and laws, every action becomes sublimated into a channel of communion, into an act of worship. The Jew can thus achieve spiritual victory without doing violence to human nature, without hermit-like fleeing from the world, without sealing his senses hermetically to the beauties and blessings of life.

V.
THE TORAH AS JEWRY'S SHIELD

The double impact of economic struggle and the unceasing assaults on the Jews should have destroyed us long ago. But the Law has been our shield and defender. The seventh day Sabbath, with its prohibition to engage in any kind of work, with its insistence that the Jew keep away from business, business thought, and from all mechanical devices, establishes for the Jew a day of a different attitude, and affords him tremendous protection against the life-destroying strain of the industrial age. Family life so arranged as to retain woman's self-respect and freedom in marriage, family worship, home celebrations, all strengthen his Jewish integration. The dietary laws not only enhance G-d-consciousness, they also help to prevent intermarriage, the safest and speediest way to racial suicide.

VI.
THE LIFE IN THE TORAH

There may be a notion in the minds of the uninitiated that the ceremonies and symbols constitute indeed a great burden. Such minds do not sufficiently appreciate the fact that these customs and observances are trained into the child's mind and life from early infancy, so that they become its natural environment.

The nearest analogy would be the Oxford and Cambridge training, one major purpose of which is to produce gentlemen. There are a number of Cambridge customs, attitudes, observances which a Cambridge man would normally and naturally retain or perform and the suggestions of which would continue to exercise an encouraging, a pleasing and also a definitely spiritual influence on him.

The Oxford man will not feel selfishly proud of his training, but he will look upon it as a special opportunity which is his special responsibility, to spread, in the most intelligent, effective manner, the ideals of his Alma Mater.

So does the Jew welcome and hail with native expectant joy the thousand and one intimate touches and suggestions of the Jewish life which are his abiding, living commentary to Judaism.

ON THE WINGS OF NIGHT

By
AARON KELLNER

In the darkness there loomed before me the tall, shadowy mass of a tenement. Silhouetted against the night sky, the building appeared cold and grim, except where here and there a lighted window gleamed and blinked like the eye of some weird monster. In the darkness, the gray brick walls appeared like huge levees, between whose bounds flowed\ the river of life, at times seething and whirling in turbulent rapids and at times flowing calm and deep and crystal clear. Behind those very walls the stream was rushing on swiftly and silently, carrying with it its human driftwood which, at the end of the long journey, it would cast wearily into the sea.

I entered the tenement and found myself in a long corridor flanked by two rows of doors. These doors—blank slabs of wood—were all outwardly identical, yet each was the curtain to a different stage, and behind each a different scene from the eternal drama of life was being enacted. Behind each door, life ebbed and flowed, yet outwardly one could hardly discern a ripple. How fascinating, I thought, to brush aside the curtain for a moment and glimpse the life that throbbed beneath!

I walked down the corridor, chose a door at random, opened it quietly, and entered. I found myself in a brilliantly lighted room with sleekly dressed men and painted women. The air was full of loud, boisterous voices and coarse laughter. On all sides I saw gayety, merriment, and carousing. Lithe young bodies were swaying and whirling to a barbaric rhythm. The movement gradually gained momentum, until it became a frenzied revel. Faster and faster beat the music; faster and yet faster whirled the dancers, until sweat stood out on their foreheads, their nostrils dilated, and their eyes bulged. The room became hot. The noise of blaring music and stamping feet grew louder and louder until it seemed that the very gates of Hell had burst and spewed its

vile brood on earth. The mad orgy sickened me. I turned and left.

Proceeding a little farther down the corridor, I was attracted toward another door by familiar strains of music. Again the same feeling of mystery and curiosity seized me. I entered silently and unseen. The room was dark except for one corner, where a lamp cast a soft light and illuminated the features of a youth of about twenty. He sat motionless, staring fixedly into the darkened corner from which the beautiful strains seemed to emanate. There was a strange familiarity about the music. In a flash I recognized it—Beethoven's immortal Fifth. The youth's lips were parted in rapture. He was oblivious of his surroundings; he was conscious only of that harmony, that divine harmony that stirred the soul to its innermost depths. The music had now an ineffable sweetness and now a roaring fury. It seemed like some vast ocean: its heaving bosom now rolling in long gentle swells, now rising into towering combers that crashed with a deafening roar. Above the surging waves, the sunlight played upon the flying spray and filled the air with flashing rainbows. In the rising crescendo of sound could be felt the spirit of man struggling to the heights, baring his breast in defiance of the fury of the elements. The music depicted the titanic struggle of man, and culminated in a stirring song of victory. The sheer beauty of the music thrilled the youth; it bore him aloft far from the pollutions of earth. He jumped up and paced back and forth ecstatically. All his being appeared suffused with a glowing warmth. For one ecstatic moment he seemed happy, supremely happy. I slipped out as silently as I had entered.

Again I found myself in the corridor viewing the row of doors, and again I reflected upon the unfathomable human secrets that each concealed. I softly opened a third door. A touching scene greeted my eyes. A mother was tenderly lulling her babe to sleep. The dimpled child, its cheeks tinted with the color of dawn, cooed softly. That sweet innocent little face seemed to symbolize all that was pure and simple and good. Its smile seemed to radiate peace and serenity. The mother looked tenderly into the eyes of her little one, the precious burden that was her flesh, her blood, her life. She rocked it gently and sang a plaintive lullaby. Her voice was wistful, with a touch of sadness in it as she visualized the future of her child, a sadness mingled with hope. The infant closed its eyes. The mother pressed it lovingly to her bosom, kissed it gently, and laid it to sleep. A tear trickled down my cheek as I softly closed the door behind me.

I walked along reflecting upon the beautifully touching scene I had just witnessed, when, from a neighboring apartment, there came muffled sobs, as if from some body racked with pain. I entered. I had just witnessed the rosy dawn of life; and now I witnessed the black night of death. The grim spectre of death still hovered about the room where his icy breath had just snuffed out a flickering candle. There lay a body that had once pulsed and throbbed with life, now rigid, cold, and dead. Ringing laughter silenced forever. No more to see the flush of dawn or the glow of sunset. That which had once thrilled to the light of day was now enshrouded in darkness and oblivion. An unseemly peace, a strange silence hovered about the dead. Death seemed so sweet, a long unbroken dream, a dream from which there was no waking, an eternal sleep. About me there was a scene of heartrending grief. Loved ones moved about dazed, their tear-filled eyes staring blankly into space. Their cruelly lacerated hearts were numb with pain; their

bodies shook with sobs. Their loss was great, irretrievable, and they gave vent to their utter despair in bitter tears. The grave would soon swallow its own, and time—the great healer—would soon mend their torn hearts. Life must go on, heedless of those who fall by the wayside. The thought came to me that we are all marked men on whom the slow, sure doom falls, pitiless and dark. The dead are dead, and we, the dying, must live on. I heaved a long drawn-out sigh, cast a last look at the bereaved and at the dead, and slowly closed the door behind me.

My head was bowed and my heart was heavy as I emerged into the street. My mind was aflame, a seething turmoil. What I had seen seemed like a meaningless confusion, a fantastic dream. One heart was warm with ecstasy, another numb with pain; some were sunk in a mad revel, others tasted of the sweet bliss of childhood. The song of life was mingled with the wail of death. I groped vainly for meaning: Nothing! Nothing! I gazed up at the stars twinkling so far above me. Here men lived and suffered and died, yet the stars smiled serenely and undisturbed, just as they had smiled down for ages upon countless generations of men. We were but insignificant creatures lost somewhere upon a tiny speck in the cosmos. Our joys and pains were but imperceptible ripples upon the vast sea of time. The eternal surge of time and tide swept on cold and inexorable. We were being ruthlessly hurled into the black abyss of oblivion by the eternal whirl of matter. A feeling of utter helplessness, of emptiness and futility gnawed at my heart, as I drifted away into the night.

Germany and the Jewish Question

By

DR. SOLOMON FLINK

AUTHOR'S NOTE: *The following study con-
cerns itself, as the title indicates, with the
Jewish Question. While the author has no
intention of denying the great contributions
of the German people to the advancement of
science, industry, and intellect, these considerations had in no way any influence on
this analysis nor on its conclusions.*

Strange as it may sound, Germany's acceptance
of submission to the Hitlerite regime and its doctrines of unrelenting race-hatred mark not a revolution, but rather a return to her pre-war ideology.
The term "revolution" connotes a radical change
in the political or intellectual beliefs of a people.
Hitler's ascension to power, however, signifies merely the "re-awakening" of the German people to
their continuous if intermittently lulled attitude of
Jew-hatred.

One cannot understand the recent outbreaks of
savagery and brutality visited upon German Jewry,
and their deeper implications, unless they be viewed
in an historical perspective.

Anti-Semitism has long been a dominant trait
of the German people. During the Middle-Ages
it was concentrated on the objections to Judaism as
a faith. Since the middle of the nineteenth century, the emphasis has been placed upon racial anti-
Semitism.

It remained for Richard Wagner, who owed
much of his success to his Jewish sponsors, to intro-
duce anti-Semitism as a racial issue into Germany.
His book, "Jews in Music" (1859) is the feeble
attempt of a physical midget who imagined himself a giant to rid himself of his moral debts to
an "inferior race." One year later, an unknown
writer, H. Nordman, published a volume, "The
Jews and the German State," denouncing the Jew
as a destructive influence in the political and eco-

nomic life of Germany. This book would be of
little historical interest were it not for the fact that
Lothar Bucher, one of its collaborators, became
later one of the close advisers of Bismarck. Perhaps, this fact helps to explain partly the abrupt
return of Bismarck to reactionary policies in 1878
and his sudden opposition to the Liberal Party,
which numbered many outstanding Jews in its
ranks.

It was during the two decades, 1878-1900,
that racial anti-Semitism reached its peak in Germany. In 1878, W. Marr wrote a pamphlet,
"Victory of Judaism over Germanism," which
within the short space of one year had more than
eleven editions. The average German found in
these utterances of the "great minds"—Gœthe,
Schopenhauer, Treitschke, Hegel, Wagner, and
others—a confirmation of his cherished racial superiority complex.

In 1880, the racial feeling became so strong
that a petition, signed by over 250,000 voters and
demanding the abrogation of the civil rights granted
to the Jews in the Act of 1812, was submitted to
Bismarck. For reasons of political expediency the
petition was disregarded by the latter. During the
next two decades, Germany was deluged with a
flood of pamphlets, denouncing the Jew as a para-
site, unworthy of German citizenship, and a menace
to Germanic culture. Court chaplain Stoecker, V.
Sonnenberg, Foerster, and others preached these
doctrines to the masses. In 1889, the above
named organized the "German-Social Party" (not
to be confused with the German Socialist party),
which adopted anti-Semitism as the main plank
of its platform. Its aims were fundamentally the
same as those of the present National-Socialist-
Labor-Party of Germany (Nazis). Within a few
years, after its foundation, this party had already
twelve deputies in the German Reichstag. The

sudden wave of prosperity which swept over Germany at the beginning of the twentieth century dimmed the flame of anti-Semitism, but never completely extinguished it.

While it is true that a number of Jews occupied prominent places in the intellectual and industrial life of Germany, it must be borne in mind that these Jews gained their position in spite of the presence of race-hatred rather than because of its absence. It is a matter of serious thought if we consider the fact that out of 380 Jewish lecturers in German universities no less than 167 had forsaken their faith before obtaining their appointment. Needless to mention the fact that in pre-war Germany, Jews were excluded from the higher positions in the military, civil, and diplomatic service.

Applying the standards of equality and liberty, as found in England, Italy, Holland in pre-war Europe, it may safely be said that German Jewry never enjoyed the civil rights granted to them in the Constitution. To Teutonism the Jew has always been the personification of sinister forces; he was viewed as an alien to the true German spirit, and a menace to Teutonic "culture." It was fully in accordance with the perverted racial superiority complex of the German people that every outstanding accomplishment of German Jews was seized upon as the most damning evidence of the attempts of the Jews to dominate German culture, intellect, or industry.

Although the creation of the German Republic in 1918 promised to exterminate racial anti-Semitism, it failed in this task for the same reasons which caused it to lose its fight against the reactionary forces.

During the first few years after the war, political adventurers like Ludendorff, Kapp, Luettwitz, Hitler, and others met with little response in their attempts to incite the masses against the Republic and against the Jews. The memories of the real events leading to the military defeat of Germany and the breakdown of the Empire were still too vivid among the people. The blunders of German diplomacy and the obstinacy and arrogance of her military leaders were still remembered by the masses. With the passage of time, however, the cold facts of reality gave way to emotional reminiscences. The various classes of the population sought relief for their particular problems. It is at this juncture, that Hitler resumed his game of political opportunism unparalleled in any other country.

Having lost their sense of reality, these classes became an easy prey to the agitator Hitler. Each group, in turn, was promised that its problems would be solved first and in a way which appealed very strongly to its own desires. Thus, the industrialists were promised the repudiation of reparations and the abolition of Trade-Unions. The farmers were promised the redistribution of the large estates and a high protective tariff wall. The laborers were lured into the Nazi camp by the assurance that unemployment would be abolished, industries would be taken over by the government, food would be obtainable at low prices, and a high standard of living would be secured. The small store owners received the pledge that department stores and chain shops would be abolished. The intellectuals and professionals were to become again the real leaders of Germany.

Each group secretly hoped that, in due time, it would be able to eliminate those features of the program which conflicted with its own interests. Hitler's great strength lies in his ability to play off all classes against one another and to keep them all in check by the magic word "nationalism." Recent events show that Hitler has fully succeeded in this direction. But it must also be apparent that a reconstructive policy cannot be based upon so conflicting a platform. And it may be added that thus far Hitler has failed completely to reveal any direct program of governmental policies.

Although the economic upheaval caused by the last war was largely responsible for the growth of the Nazi movement, it would be erroneous to ascribe the subsequent development to economic factors alone. Two decades characterized alternately by war, inflation, dislocation of industry, temporary prosperity, depression and far-spread unemployment have left their marks upon the psychology of the German people. The youth of 1914, which represents Germany's manhood of today, has forgotten, if it ever possessed, those traits for which the German was universally respected prior to 1914. The youth of Germany has lost the ambition and the ability to start at the bottom. Instead it prefers to dream of days gone by and to hope that some political miracle will enable them to awake one morning and to call the past a freakish nightmare.

Hand in hand with the economic disturbances went this radical change in the social structure of Germany and the philosophy of life of its citizens. A proper appraisal of these changes is indispensable for a proper understanding of the historical development.

In the case of Germany, such an analysis must start with the intellectual and professional classes. Prior to the Great War, a university diploma was the magic key which opened to its possessor the gates to a promising career. The leading positions in governmental service as well as in private industry were reserved for the "doctor." Such a title, or the meaningless adjective "von" or "Baron," was sufficient to compensate for intellectual deficiencies or lack of proper qualifications.

Self-contentment and blind patriotism were the chief traits of the middle class. To obtain a meaningless "title" or third-class order was the most cherished ambition of its members. In the ordinary course of life this class took little interest in politics. Such matters were left to the "leaders"; the citizen, or to use the more appropriate term, the "civilian" had to "obey." The same analysis applies to the farmer and the laborer. Altho the Socialist party had grown in strength in the pre-war period, its chief aim was to obtain some economic concessions for the working masses.

After 1918, the philosophy of these classes underwent a radical change. The loss of class prestige, position, or wealth led to a greater interest in party politics. University students found their diplomas alone of little aid in their search of employment. The pre-war glamour of student

days had given way to the dire necessity of hard and intensive study in preparation for life's grim battle. The labor class found itself suddenly at the helm of the government. But the long bred inferiority complex caused it to hesitate in using its power. The Republic graciously overlooked the antipathy of its servants to the existing form of government. It cherished the hope to gradually gain their support for the new Germany. On the other hand, the peasants suffered from their inability to compete against foreign producers whose methods of cultivation were far superior. The middle class had lost most of its savings during the inflation (1919-1923) and was no longer the "pillar" of the Empire.

Seizing upon this gradual estrangement of these groups from the Republic, the industrialists and intellectuals began to re-assert their reactionary doctrines. University professors turned into fierce, fanatical lecturers, demanding a return of Germany to her old institutions. Government employees openly allied themselves with the anti-Republican cause, at first with the Nationalists and later with the Nazis. Leaders of business and industry attacked the social policies of the Republic. Students demanded their "natural" right to the best positions by virtue of their diplomas. The middle-class asked for the restoration of its lost fortunes and mourned the loss of the Imperial glamour.

Thus, slowly but surely, the German Republic neared its end. After the depression of 1930 made itself felt in Germany, the Republic was doomed, unless it was willing to fight. The masses hesitated and the battle was lost. In a series of articles which appeared in the "Jewish Forum" more than two years ago, the author for the first time called attention to the inevitable rise of Hitler to power in such an eventuality.

The unchecked growth of the Nazi movement thus appears as an inevitable historical development. It is also clear why the anti-Semitic platform of Hitler was so readily accepted by the German population. Each of the various classes had its own "grievance" against the Republic. To each one of these groups, Hitler had promised the relief they wanted. That the persecution and eventual extermination of the Jews in Germany was part of Hitler's program was no deterrent factor, because, as has been stated above, the average - German had always viewed the Jew as an alien. Hindenburg, von Papen, Luther, and all other leading Germans were little concerned with the fate of the Jew. To them "German culture" meant "German" first, and "culture" was a secondary matter. After all, did not Hindenburg himself state on one occasion that he has never read a single book outside of military literature?

Although only an innocent bystander in this struggle for political supremacy, German Jewry became the center of controversy. It is needless to reiterate, here, all the accusations hurled by Hitler against the Jews. Every evil that had befallen Germany was attributed to the sinister conspiracies of the Jewish race.

German Jewry failed in the critical hour of its history to combat anti-Semitism. Instead of fighting its adversaries, it denied their existence. And it will forever remain a blot upon German Jewry that for many years past it attempted to shift the brunt of anti-Semitism to the relatively few and extremely harmless Jews who had immigrated from Eastern Europe; the anti-Semitic outbursts in the second half of the last century were directed against *German* Jews. It should be emphasized that it was General Ludendorff himself who, during the last war, in his proclamation— "An meine gelibten Yidden in Paulan" (To my beloved Jews in Poland)—had invited these Jews to come to Germany, where they would find a haven of refuge. The author has spent the greater part of his life in Germany and has never found any evidence of foreign Jews who were prominent members of the Socialist or Communist parties in Germany. Only a small fraction of the many thousands who had come to Germany succeeded in obtaining German citizenship. Some of them gained wealth, the majority, however, remained small shopkeepers, peddlers, artisans, or merchants.

At the same time it must be stated that the masses of the German Jews lacked the idealism and spirituality which would have enabled them to combat anti-Semitism in its earlier stages. The assimilation movement among German Jewry was not caused by a desire to find a compromise between the requirements of Mosaic Law and modern civilization. It was rather due to an ill-concealed attempt to delegate Jewishness, and all that it implies, into an inconspicuous corner. German Jews have never recognized the spiritual bonds which unite the Jews in all foreign lands. Instead of fighting anti-Semitism, they overemphasized their Germanism and their devotion, often overstepping the boundaries of decency and self-respect. Thus, about a year ago, the German Nationalist Jews, under the leadership of Naumann, proffered their alliance to Hitler and expressed their desire to organize a Nazi troop of their own. Such tactics were ill-suited as weapons against the vortex of race-hatred.

It is one of the inexplicable ironies of history that the "super"-German Jews were the first to feel the fist of Hitler. Dr. Bernard Weiss, former vice-president of the Prussian police force, stated in a speech in 1928 that all foreign Jews are undesirable elements and that the German population has never been anti-Jewish. And Dr. Bernard Weiss was the first Jewish office-holder who had to flee Germany in fear of the Nazis. Another illustration is the case of Dr. Kurt Soelling, who abandoned his faith, and became a member of the German Supreme Court. Shortly after Hitler's ascension to power, Dr. Soelling advised the removal of Jewish judges from the criminal courts to civil courts. And again, it was Dr. Soelling who was the first "Jewish" judge to be removed from the bench.

The future of Germany is, indeed, gloomy and pregnant with grave dangers for the peace of Europe. The primitive instincts of savagery and brutality revived among the masses by Hitler spell grave dangers for peace, unless efficient and quick action be taken by the leading powers. Already at this juncture, it appears that Hitler is no longer the "leader," but rather the mouthpiece of the in-

(Continued on Page 59)

Sonnets to Revissa

By

BERNARD DOV MILIANS

I.

Death knocked one evening as you lay asleep
  And called to you to follow silently;
I did not hear the sombre angel sweep
  Away, with you, our joyful harmony.
I heard the scream which I had heard before,
  It deafened me—I shuddered and I shrank—
Was it imagination and no more
  That froze my soul and left my mind a blank?

How well I saw your bitter waxen smile,
  The glassy stare that peered beyond the sky,
I cried: O mother, yet remain a while,
  Much rather fate had willed that I should die!
Now you are gone, but still you shed a light
  That luminates the sadness of the night.

II.

Forgive me, mother, if in sad lament
  I should disturb your everlasting peace;
A stubborn destiny will not relent,
  And with grim smile it sees my woe increase.
O tell me, from your macrocosmic world
  How can I best avoid the precipice
Whence, through the ages, millions have been
    hurled
  By fate's command and Cupid's artifice?

I square my shoulders, I am not afraid,
  One moment I would dare to face a king,
The next my head is bowed, I am dismayed
  And cry that death should leave its poisoned
    sting.
But oftentimes, although my head is bowed,
  My rebel soul stands firm and is not cowed.

III.

The moon and stars were shielded by a cloud
  And groaning night-winds chilled the dismal air.
The dreamer stood alone and wept, aloud—
  He wept—and of the world was unaware.
Then suddenly he recognized a sound,
  A muffled whisper scarcely audible,
That grew as it approached, until it drowned
  The noisy wind that seemed implacable.

A flash of lightning cut the sky in two
  With roaring, rumbling thunder in its wake
The heavens cried, their tears were blown askew,
  And mother Earth herself began to quake.
The dreamer heard—and sighing, bent his head,—
  "*You must accept!*" was counselled by the dead.

EDITORIAL STAFF—(Sitting l. to r.) Aaron Kellner, Israel E. Friedman, Abraham S. Guterman, Jacob Agushewitz, Hyman A. Israel. (Standing l. to r.) Isaac Goldberg, Sidney Nissenbaum, Leo J. Usdan, Moses Feuerstein, William Kaufman, Bernard D. Milians.

EDITORIAL STAFF

ABRAHAM S. GUTERMAN
Editor-in-Chief

Associates

JACOB AGUSHEWITZ   HYMAN A. ISRAEL

AARON KELLNER

Art Editor   *Typographical Editor*
BERNARD D. MILIANS   ISAAC GOLDBERG

BUSINESS STAFF

Business Manager   *Asst. Business Mgr.*
ISRAEL E. FRIEDMAN   LEO J. USDAN

Advertising Managers
SIDNEY NISSENBAUM
MOSES FEUERSTEIN

WILLIAM KAUFMAN—*Asst. Advertising Mgr.*

The Second Generation

By

Hyman A. Israel

The pale drawn face of George Hartman is at variance with the harmony created by the moonlit waves, the music from the ship's ballroom and the lovers at the railing. Slowly he paces the deck, his hands clasped behind him. He is being borne rapidly toward the realization of his life-long dream, but his mind pulls him backward in hesitation.

In his childhood Hartman had thrilled to stories of Biblical heroes, and the hills and valleys of his fathers had filled his day dreams. In his youth, the calmness of his Talmudic studies had been shattered by the intrusion of Occidental thought into his-little world. Zionism had stepped into the breach, healing his wounds and proclaiming for him with commanding eloquence the road forward.

The cultural writers of the movement spoke of the soul of the race which stretched like a Thesean cord through the labyrinthine windings of the people's history. This racial soul it was which determined the peculiar contribution of the Jews to the world's civilization. Centuries of exile and oppression had stifled the creative powers of the race, and its members had all but forgotten its soul and purpose. But now the race was awakening. Cultural emancipation had cast it upon the swirling waters of modern thought and creation. It was looking upon itself and into itself. It was searching its past for the secret of its existence; and soon the thread of its soul would be caught up again. In the freedom of its ancient homeland, the Jewish race would again create, and its creations would take their place among the works of the nations. Young Hartman heard and was impressed.

The pogroms of his native Russia drove Hartman as a young man to seek refuge in America. His diligent application soon gained him recognition in the business circles of his mid-Western city.

He married and had a son. But he did not forget the national homeland. He was vexed by the lukewarm interest in Zionism manifested by the American-born Jews of his acquaintance. He was certain that his attachment to the movement was well-founded, and was resolved that his son, Arthur, should see the logic of his views. No pains were spared in carrying out this resolution. Hebrew-speaking tutors and a trip to Palestine aroused the boyish enthusiasm to such a pitch that the father no longer doubted that he and his son were of one accord.

When Arthur went away to college, Hartman felt a half conscious fear that all would not be well. The college was one of the largest institutions in the East, and breathed a decidedly international atmosphere. The boy wrote home, however, that he had joined a Zionist club, and that was enough to allay the father's fears. All went smoothly the first two years. The young man spent the summers at home in his father's business. Although he had lost his boyish enthusiasm, he still showed an active interest in Jewish problems and Zionist activities. During the third year, he did indeed change the tone of his letters, but Hartman did not take the change seriously. He attributed it to the fact that certain new fields were being opened to the boy. The latter was enthusiastic about psychology, economics, and social problems. He wrote of visits to social institutions. He had joined in a students' strike against the suppression by the authorities of a liberal publication. The father thought that this was but a passing whim of a growing adolescent. "Another year will pass and he will settle down again."

At the end of the third year, the boy's mother died. The death was naturally a blow to both father and son, but Hartman felt in addition a sense of freedom. Now there was nothing in the way of his settling in Palestine, nothing to hold him further in America. Of course, his son would go with him. The father felt sure of it, although the topic had not been discussed by them of late. He had purposely refrained from bringing it up, for fear Arthur might feel that it was in opposition to some newly-found interests, and might react emotionally against it. "Better wait until the boy finishes college."

The son went back to complete his studies; the father set about to dispose of his business and to close his accounts.

*　*　*

Hartman sinks down into a deck chair and his blank gaze sees nothing of the moonlit sea toward which it is directed. Once again he is recalling that evening in his son's little library. He doesn't seem to be able to sweep that scene from his mind. It was the evening after the young man's return from his graduation exercises. Arthur had gone to his library to write some letters. Hartman had come in and broached the question of the future. As he reviews that scene, he remembers that Arthur was calm and self-contained, whereas for the first time in years he, Hartman, felt himself disturbed and excited. Arthur spoke in even tones and without emotion. He had suspected that his father was planning to go to Palestone. He had expected to be asked to go also, and had given the matter careful consideration—he had tried to be fair to both his father and himself. But he coud not consider settling permanently in Palestine.

"I shall always be interested in Palestine. A new life is awakening there, and its development will be of interest, but so will a new life be created by the Jews of America. This talk about the soul of the race expressing itself more purely in Palestine is unintelligble to me. Will Palestinian science be more scientific than American science? Will Palestinian social values be of a higher quality than the social values that the American Jews will set up? Who will be the judge between them? Will there be such a thing as a Palestinian philosophy, uninfluenced by the knowledge and thought of the rest of the world? What is the nature of the Jewish racial soul? In our history we find

movements that range from extreme mysticism to extreme rationalism. Which of these movements was more Jewish than the others? The customs and family life of the Jews of Yemen are different than the customs and family life of the Jews of America. When the Jews of Germany were engaged in Talmudic researches, the Jews of Spain were writing love songs and studying Plato. Were the ones motivated by a more Jewish soul than the others, or were they merely human beings with a common past reacting to different conditions of environment.

"I can feel a brotherly relationship to the oppressed Jews of all countries, for their oppressors assume the existence of a Jewish race soul, which puts all Jews the world over in the same category in their opinion. If I happened to be present at the times of Jewish persecutions, I too would suffer equally. But must I, because my enemies persecute me on the basis of certain assumptions, proclaim those assumptions to be true? No, father, let's not be so prone to let our wishes influence our thoughts. It is convenient for the individual who seeks greater safety with some particular group to feel that there is some innate soul which binds the members of the group into an indissoluble brotherhood. But it does not follow that such is the case. Our desire for immortality leads us to cherish the thought that the particular stream in which our life is flowing springs from some eternally-unquenchable fountainhead and will flow forever. I am content to view my desires calmly and to satisfy myself with a smaller portion of immortality.

"You want to go to Palestine and I believe it is the best thing you can do. You were not reared in America as I was, and its ways and institutions cannot be a part of you as they are a part of me. In Palestine you will find companionship and rest. You will find there men with past experiences common to yours, whose spirits can secure rest only in Palestine. I must remain here. My childhood and youth have been spent here. My problems are the problems of young Amer-

(*Continued on Page* 69)

Principles in the Philosophy of Hermann Cohen

By

RABBI JACOB AGUSHEWITZ

The philosophy of Hermann Cohen is profoundly important in the general field of culture, as well as in the more specialized field of Jewish knowledge. In general philosophy, Hermann Cohen founded a new school, known as Neo-Kantianism, or Critical Idealism. In an age which was torn between the two extremes of mysticism and materialism, he ushered in the movement "back to Kant" which has since become the dominant philosophy in Germany. Into the philosophy of Judaism, too, Hermann Cohen infused new vitality. His posthumous work, "The Religion of Reason from Jewish Sources," has been hailed in many circles as second only to Maimonides' "Guide." Cohen's views of Judaism are especially interesting as they do not spring out of the desire to reconcile Judaism and philosophy. To him, there is no philosophy to be contrasted with Judaism. On the contrary, true philosophy leads to Judaism and finds its symbolic and most profound expression in Jewish literature and practices.

In this article, the attempt is made to outline the fundamental principles of Cohen's system, so as to prepare the reader for, and create an interest in, a closer study of his works, and the writings of the many distinguished thinkers who consider themselves disciples of this great Jewish philosopher.

I.

Perhaps the most convenient standpoint from which to survey the system of Hermann Cohen is the one of human values. In a world of inexorable mechanical laws, where ethics and religion seem at best to be but the helpless cravings of the human soul, the echoes of "an infant crying for the light," Cohen undertakes to re-establish the independence and essential significance of those noble aspirations. Ethical, religious and æsthetic values are threatened in the modern world not so much by lack of appreciation, as by the irresistible desire to explain and understand. The attitude which has proven so successful in the scientific investigations of nature has proven harmful when carried over to the realm of human values.

Ethical values came to be explained in terms of instincts and early training. Thus, the feeling of duty is explained by materialists as the outgrowth of child life. A child depends largely on its parents. Its self-assertive instinct is thus partially inhibited, and in the adult, this feeling of compulsion, of the inhibition of his own will, rises in consciousness as the feeling of duty. Pity, mercy and æsthetic appreciation are interpreted as due to the projection of ourselves into the external world. The "happy ending" in a novel is proverbially desired, for the reader tends to identify himself with the hero of the story. The sight of healthy persons delights our mind, whereas that of suffering people depresses our spirit—a feeling interpreted in consciousness as pity or mercy. Religious values are similarly explained as due to fear, the sublimation of sexual instincts and the projection of the will to live into the future.

Obviously, explanations of this sort cannot satisfy the moral or religious consciousness. Instead of interpreting ethical and religious values as signs of degeneracy or decay, the human mind, at least that of civilized people, considers them as being the expression of its highest aspirations and aims.

Shall we conclude, then, that the methods of science fail when applied to human beings? For it was apparently the scientific method that the materialists employed for the explanation of human values. Science seems to consider an event as explained when it can be expressed as a rearrangement of unchanging particles. The formation of new compounds in chemistry were unexplained until, by the aid of atomic theory, they were understood as merely the rearrangement of its component atoms. Similarly, in psychology, the self-assertive principle is taken as the element, all the other psychic events being complications and modifications of the same principle.

It is not as if all wishes need be logically deduced from the self assertive principle or the will to live, for then the so-called human values would require another principle of explanation. The will to live may, however, be conditioned—that is, combined with certain experiences to produce a novel product. Thus, the "higher values" may be excrescences of the will to live, though certainly the idea of self-assertion does not *logically* lead to ethics and religion. Similarly, does not science explain color as due to waves of certain frequencies, though the idea of color does not follow from the idea of disturbances in the ether? Science seems to be satisfied with explaining water as the combination of oxygen and hydrogen, though certainly the properties of water, taste, wetness or boiling point, cannot be deduced from the properties of oxygen and hydrogen.

Materialism, then, is interested in discovering the mechanical order of the universe, rather than in constructing a logical system. In the investigations of nature as in the study of the human self, it is content to take certain things for granted, as given to us by the external world, and confines itself to the discovery of the mechanical relations obtaining among these elements. Thus, the concepts of matter, energy, motion, attraction and repulsion in physics, as the drives of self-assertion and sex in psychology, are taken as elementary facts, as "given" concepts, all events being explained, not as deducible from these concepts, but as combinations and rearrangements of them.

At this point, Hermann Cohen begins his discussion. If the world can be understood at all, he asserts, it is only as a logical order that it can be conceived. We could not infer the most elementary conclusions from a scientific experiment concerning, say, the nature of the electron, unless we subscribed to the principle that nature somehow obeys the laws of reason. Whenever we essay any proposition concerning the nature of the external world, we affirm the Parmenidean statement "Being and Thought are one." If Being and Thought are to be one, however, the constructions and laws of Thought must suffice for the understanding of Being. Thought, or Reason, contains within itself all that is necessary for its own achievements. In other words, "Pure Thought" requires nothing "given" by Nature for the understanding of Nature. Pure thought originates its own concepts out of itself, then deduces all events, not mechanically, but logically from them.

Thus, we see that Cohen removes all the bounds of reason. Not only do the constructions of reason suffice for the understanding of the world, but it is impossible to understand the world logically in any other way. There are certain forms of thought, certain conceptions "laying the foundation" (Grundlegungen) for all subsequent reasoning. Nothing can be conceived in any other way but that which follows logically from these basic concepts. These forms of thought or ideas, in the language of Cohen, can be discovered by continually reducing all logical terms to the underlying more general concepts. The fundamental most general idea is free from all "givenness;" it represents the transition from the nothing to something. Hence, the idea must establish the origin of concepts.

All the concepts which materialism employs do not suffice for Cohen, as they all bear the stamp of "givenness." Matter, energy, and the primitive instincts are not ultimate logical concepts. Their validity rests only on the fact that they are found in nature. For a thorough rationalist, these terms are, at best, advanced abstractions, not fundamental concepts. The most fundamental ideas, or forms of thought, must be limit concepts—that is, ideas representing the boundary between Being and Non-Being. To any empirically-minded opponent who refuses to grant reason such dictatorial powers, Cohen replies that to set limits to reason amounts to a confession of failure. The only ground on which two disputants can meet is the one of logic, and the one who retreats from this ground declares himself by this very act vanquished. Furthermore, the great Jewish thinker would point to mathematics as proving that the world can .be understood in thought's own terms, origin concepts only. To mathematics, then, we must turn our attention.

II.

Cohen's contention so far, then, is that it is only through the basic ideas resident in the nature of thought itself that the world can be adequately conceived. Whenever the attempt is made to explain the universe by means of concepts borrowed from the external world, an insoluble antinomy is the inevitable result. Thus, the nature of extension and motion was an insoluble problem until the development of differential analysis.

Space is conceived in the human mind as infinitely divisible. When we conceive a certain length, we can think of it as divisible in half, then in quarters, in eighths, and so on *ad infinitum*. Yet we find it impossible to go back, to build up the idea of that length out of the infinitely small particles. Shall we decide, then, that space or extension is not infinitely divisible? Shall we declare our natural propensity to divide space as an irrational, foolish drive? However the infinite divisibility of space is found not only in our mind but also in nature. Motion does not occur by leaps and bounds, but is continuous. Circular motion, in particular, must be conceived of as changing its direction in every instant of time. The direction changes at every point, though a point by definition cannot have any direction. The falling of a stone to the ground presents the same problem. The velocity of the stone is increased at every point in its path, though the path cannot be conceived as created by the continual addition of point to point.

Thus we arrive at an antinomy. Extension cannot be built out of points; yet points are imperative for the understanding of extension.

This antinomy could only be lifted by the method of differential analysis. A derivative is defined as the limiting value of the ratio

$$\frac{\text{change of } y}{\text{change of } x}$$

when change of x approaches zero. As is well known, the rate of change of the velocity of a falling body, as well as the change in direction of curvilinear motion, can be easily expressed and calculated as derivatives. Thus, the derivative does not refer to a point in space, which is defined as having no dimensions, but to an infinitesimal line approximating a point. Hence, the antinomy is removed as one may construct a line out of the derivative by the simple process of integration. The finite can be analyzed into infinitesimal quantities, then built up again from them.

Since the derivative is such a powerful instrument for the solution of philosophical and physical difficulties, let us investigate what sort of concept it is. Now, it certainly is not a given concept, one that was in the external world, as it cannot be visualized as a definite quantity nor even as a ratio of definite quantities. From the above definition of a derivative, it is evident that a derivative can only be conceived as a production of Pure Thought, a limit concept. The derivative represents the transition from a point to extension, nothing to something, from Non-Being to Being. It stands for the production of extension out of thought, quantity out of quality. Thus, the derivative is a fundamental idea, a form of thought. Hence, it is indispensable in logic as in physics. "There is no other method whereby to formulate the natural laws—nay, not alone to formulate them, but to lay the foundation for them, than the one that is firmly assured in the differential analysis." (Logic, p. 265) The discovery of the derivative marked the final establishment of Pure Thought. "This mathematical production of motion, and through it of nature, is the triumph of Pure Thought." (Logic, p. 262)

From the way the various mathematical concepts may be evolved out of the derivative, we may learn how all concepts develop out of the fundamental idea. As we saw, the concept of continuity can be derived from the derivative by the process of integration. The integrated function can be seen, given in nature, as a line, an area, or a volume. Hence, it produces the concept of the many, as any definite quantity is conceived in thought as divisible, as consisting of many quantities. Writing the integrated expression in its most general form $y=f(x)$, we can derive a series of points by assigning "x" definite values and obtaining the corresponding values for "y". In this series, every term depends on the preceding term, and conditions the following terms. Stated in this form, the function is the expression of the law of causality, for the causal principle can be thus expressed: the appearance of a certain object shows that a *definite* object had previously appeared, and that a certain *definite* object will appear at some future date. The concept of totality, too, is derived from the mathematical series, for the summation of an infinite series like $1 + \frac{1}{2} + \frac{1}{4} + \frac{1}{8} - \ldots$ cannot be conceived in thought as occurring through continual addition, but as a single act of summation, an all-togetherness, totality concept.

Thus, the concepts of the many and totality, continuity and causality are derived from the fundamental idea, the derivative. This conclusion must not be interpreted, however, to mean that mind imposes its own categories of knowledge on nature. One must not infer from the foregoing analysis that the real world may be One, Eternal and Free, but our consciousness distorts the real world by viewing it through the accursed glasses of the Many and Causality. We must recall the most fundamental postulate of Cohen's system. Being and Thought are one; hence, Being is the being of Thought. Whatever is true in the nature of Thought is true of Being. Consequently, the categories of knowledge *are* the categories of being and it is impossible that the world should hide its real qualities from the human mind.

It is true, however, that all certainty is based on the fundamental idea. Pure Thought, not sensual experience, is the ultimate authority.* All events must fit into the logical categories of knowledge.

Hence, the world can only be known as a logical order, not a mechanical one. Mechanical explanations may be partially true—that is, correct for the sum of knowledge available. To be finally true, however, explanations must be in the form of deductions from a fundamental idea. The road to ethics and religion is thus thrown open.

———

In several places, Hermann Cohen admits that the fundamental idea may be proven false by experience, and depends for its justification on success in the realm of experience.

III.

From the study of mathematics, we concluded that the world is essentially rational. In the analysis of the ethical will, we must remember, therefore, to reject all mechanical explanations of it, as inadequate. We shall insist on the recognition of the primacy and independence of the ethical demands until they are shown to be logically derivable from animal impulses. Now, excluding religious and æsthetic values, which will be considered later, the ethical demands are essentially unlike all our other wishes or desires. While we may assign definite reasons for our desires, the ethical will must remain unexplained. We want bread to still our hunger, water to quench our thirst, certain necessities and luxuries to enhance our comfort. In short, the search for pleasure and avoidance of pain explains all our ordinary physical desires and wishes. The ethical demands, however, defy all explanations of this sort. What reason can a person have in wishing his neighbors' welfare, the success of his country, or the welfare of humanity in general? Yet such wishes often rise to the intensity of causing a person to sacrifice his life for their sake. The patriotic soldier who braves death for his country and the heroic scientist who battles the deadly microbes are impelled by a command for which they can find no reason or explanation in their own consciousness.

Having banned all psychological explanations as being of a mechanical, not a logical nature, we conclude that the ethical will is ultimate and independent of the mathematical—physical order.

Mathematics relates to the world of Being; Ethics, to the world of the Ought. (Sein and Sollen). Being and Ought are two distinct realms, each subject to different laws. Yet both realms are problems of reason, and both must be "pure," free from all givenness. Hence, in ethics, as in mathematics, we must find the fundamental idea, out of which all ethical concepts are evolved.

In investigating the nature of the ethical concepts, we first note that they all postulate the unity of personality. Conceptions like duty and responsibility have meaning only when referred to the person as a whole, and become inane terms when applied to any one of the drives, like love, anger, fear, constituting the human personality. If we consider the human personality behavioristically,— that is, as being merely the general name for the totality of one's emotions and impulses, the ethical conceptions refer only to some human tendencies, not to the person as a whole. We can, then, no more think of the person as responsible for the expression of any of his impulses than we can blame the elements of nature for their indifference to human weal or woe. Hence, the very existence of ethics demands the unity of the self. Action must be considered as expressing the will of the entire personality, not merely of the impulses which happened to gain the ascendancy for the moment.

At this point, we may recall the traditional solution of this difficulty. The ancient and medieval philosophers thought of the soul-substance as the substratum of all human activity in the same manner as matter is the substratum of all physical manifestations. Thus, the variety of human impulses was considered as the expression of the underlying, unifying soul. Accordingly, ethical demands were always referred to the soul, which could be held responsible for all the actions of the personality. In spite of the attractiveness of this theory, however, critical idealism is forced to reject it. The soul-substance is a "given" concept, one that is supposedly found in experience. Hence, it cannot form the basis of an ethics of "pure will," which can only begin with the productions of pure thought.

In our studies in logic, we referred to mathe-

maties for the purpose of finding the fundamental idea, which generates all the physical concepts. In the investigation of ethics, we may turn to a science which stands in the same relation to ethics as mathematics is to logic, namely: the science of jurisprudence. Now, in the science of law, will is often attributed, not only to a person, but to a group of persons. Thus, a corporation is considered a legal personality. The will of a corporation is as responsible in the eyes of the law as the will of a single person, though the will of the former is really constituted of a number of wishes. Will, too, is often attributed to the state, though it is really many wills, being at best only the expression of the majority of its citizens. The possibility of these wills in thought suggests the existence of a fundamental idea of unity, molding many impulses in the conception of one will. Thus, the idea of the will of the whole as being a unity springs into existence.

Applying this fundamental idea to the human personality, we can think of the ethical concepts as referring to the will of the whole person, though, from a causal point of view, action may be the result of one impulse gaining the ascendancy over the other ones. In doing so, we are not consciously blinding ourselves to the facts; on the contrary, we are following the fundamental ethical form of thought. No group of persons could have been declared as a legal personality without the basic ethical idea of unity. Furthermore, all ethical thought becomes self-contradictory when this fundamental idea is abandoned, just as all thought concerning the physical world led to antinomies when the fundamental mathematical idea, the derivative, was ignored.

Having produced the idea of pure will out of thought, we next come to the evolution of less general concepts out of it. Now, the idea of will obviously refers us to the concept of man. From our studies in logic, however, we learned that concepts develop out of unity, through the many, to totality. The concept of man, accordingly, must also undergo these developments. The individual stage is the completely selfish one, in which the person seeks his own good only. Gradually, the person comes to identify his self with his family, then his tribe, his nation, his race and eventually, with his state. These stages are incarnations of the concept of man as extending beyond the physical individual to embrace "many" persons. The ultimate grade, the final expression of pure will, is the one of totality, wherein the person considers all of humanity as being part of himself.

Thus, the ethical self is conceived as a task, not as a given substratum. All of our ethical actions lead to the ethical self, surmount an obstacle in the eternal road, which leads to the realization of altruism and cosmopolitanism.* The Good to which our moral consciousness strives is far beyond our reach; yet, our good actions tend to bring us closer and closer to the ultimate goal. Right is that action which brings us closer to the identification of ourselves with the rest of humanity; wrong, the action which tends to veer us away from this goal.

Ethical values are thus reared on the foundation of the idea of pure will, just as the understanding of physical phenomena is based on the idea of the derivative. Far from being impaired, the certainty of both sciences is enhanced by being based on thought, rather than on sensation. For, are not the sure and permanent principles of logic superior to the fleeting impressions of our senses? Yet, the human consciousness remains dissatisfied. It demands the establishment of a definite relation between the realm of Being and the realm of Ought. After all, human actions occur in the mathematico-physical world. The attitude of nature then determines the possibility of the realization of the ethical self. The hostility, or even the indifference of nature, reduces the moral command to a call in the wild, a "voice in the wilderness." Hence, the realization of the ethical self demands the existence of another fundamental idea, expressing the relation between Being and Ought.

Cohen finds the certainty of ethical progress in the idea of truth, or G-d. In logic, we deal with concepts like necessity, generality, correctness, but not with truth. The idea of truth can only refer

to the connection between logic and ethics, to the fact that both sciences are based on fundamental ideas. Truth, then, applies to the method of searching, finding truth. "The search of truth, that alone is truth." The ethical aspect of the idea of truth is the idea of G-d. His existence insures the permanent relation between Being and Ought. "Nature is preserved for ethics."

The classical ethical doctrines of human immortality and free will are interpreted in accordance with this doctrine of the nature of G-d. By the striving of the ethical self for immortality is meant the assurance that there will always be an external world in which the ethical self could be realized. Freedom of will, too, can only mean that in the eternal march to the Good, there will never be a time when the human individual will be a means only.

In short, ethics is based on the fundamental idea of Pure Will. Its completion, however, demands the existence of G-d, who links Being with Ought. Faith in G-d is the expression in consciousness of the ethical will.

As the essence of religion is the relation between G-d and man, the ground is now laid for the Religion of Reason.

IV.

In the previous chapters, we have sketched the outlines of Cohen's logic and ethics. The fields of thinking and willing have thus been investigated. As the realm of feeling is reserved for æsthetics, it would seem that no place was left for religion. Indeed, Cohen concludes that the field of religion cannot be granted any independence,—that is, religion is not evolved out of a fundamental idea. Religion does have, however, a content peculiarly its own, which justifies its inclusion within the system (nicht Selbststaendigkeit sondern Eigenart).

Religion differs from ethics in referring to the individual. The ethical self is not concerned about the failure of any particular person; it is interested mainly in the success of the whole. Religion, however, appears in the contrite repentance of the individual. When an individual becomes conscious of having trespassed an ethical law, he begins to feel like a castaway, one that was left behind in the universal march of progress. In his dejection, he turns to G-d for help. Now, G-d does not, by a miraculous gesture, turn a sinner into a saint. That would be a violation, both of the transcedence of G-d and the autonomy of man. The idea of G-d, however, provides the assurance of ethical progress. Hence, the person who believes in G-d does not yield to despair, for he still feels himself a member of the army that is ever marching forward toward the ethical goal.

Passing now to a closer investigation of the nature of religion, we note that true religion must be monotheistic. Monotheism believes in the existence of G-d apart from nature; pantheism, on the other hand, identifies G-d and nature. As G-d in Cohen system represents the summit of all ethical striving, it is evident that identifying G-d and nature amounts to obviating all distinction between the Realm of Being and the Realm of Ought. Thus, pantheism robs ethics of its independence and significance, and true religion must be cleared of all pantheistic taints.

The Being of G-d is essentially different from he being of other things. His existence is that of the fundamental idea and His being is essentially the insurance of the progressive realization of the ethical self. Hence, G-d can only be described in ethical terms and the attribution to Him of physical qualities is the error of pantheism and mysticism, the unpardonable sin.

After surveying the various religious works, Cohen concludes that the Jewish sources reveal religion in its philosophical purity. Already in the first chapter of Genesis, the message is proclaimed that Man is the goal of creation. It is not as if the universe sprang into existence at a definite historic date, but the world is continually created, preserved by G-d for the ethical goal. The significance of the rainbow, too, as explained in Genesis, is an illustration of the true conception of G-d. G-d insures the continuation of nature for the eternal progress of ethics. Also the name of G-d, as revealed to Moses, *Eheyeh Asher Eheyeh*, shows that the future is an essential attribute to the

Being of G-d. G-d insures the future of ethics and continually leads to it.

The uniqueness of G-d's Being is continually emphasized in Jewish literature. The thirteen attributes of G-d in Exodus, are all ethical terms, and Jewish philosophers have always insisted on the interpretation of *Echad* as the "uniqueness of His unity, and the unity of His uniqueness" *Achdoth Yichudo Veyichud Achdutho*. The idea that G-d's attributes are only man's ethical tasks is beautifully embodied in the Jewish concept of Holiness. Man must strive forever to be like G-d. "And be you holy, for I am holy." Again, the famous saying of the Talmudic Sages, "Unto Him you shall cleave. As He is merciful, so must you be merciful," etc.

Prayer is the expression of the yearning of the soul after G-d, the solemn acceptance of the ethical goal. The Jewish insistence on frequent and regular prayer services is thus completely in line with the demands of the ethical consciousness.

The most profound religious insight, however, Cohen finds in the messianic ideal proclaimed by the prophets. The messianic goal is the ethical goal, is the kingdom of G-d on earth, is the reign of cosmopolitanism and absolute justice. Every day shall one wait for the coming of the Messiah, for one must continually aspire to reach the ethical self.

For the purpose of teaching the supremacy of ethics, the Jews segregated themselves from the rest of humanity by erecting the barrier of the numerous dietary laws and similar observances. As the Jewish laws have thus arisen with the only purpose of approaching the ethical goal, they are all revealed by G-d,—that is, produced by the purely ethical consciousness and necessary channels of the eternal progress of ethics.

The dispersion of the Jewish people to all ends of the earth is also fortunate from the ethical point of view, as it uprooted the last vestiges of local patriotism. "G-d tore us from our country in order to reveal it to us in humanity. To proclaim to the world the truth of the one and only G-d

(*Continued on Page 53*)

FANTASIES AND FANCIES

By

ABRAHAM S. GUTTERMAN

I.

What boots it for me to continue to live! Again and again I find myself immersed in the depths of sorrow and overwhelmed by insurmountable waves of hopelessness. Despondency reigns over me. It has driven out all the brightness of life. Sombre are its hues, shaded its colors. Its voice tears at the strings of my heart; powerful and penetrating, it demands exclusive attention. It cries forth at every occasion, at every moment, at every instant of being. Bitter are its protests, pitiful its entreaties. Its clarion calls ring in the chambers of my consciousness. It rushes screaming through my nervous system, causing my entire being to jangle in crazy vibration. To wail is futile. To curse the fates—what fates?

I bury myself in study; but to no avail. I bury myself in pleasures; but in vain. I try to suppress the blackness, to squelch it, to choke it. Constantly, never ceasing, it pours forth its plaints.

I seek the fields, the trees, the grass. I lie down on the green mattress of earth, and gaze at the blue mantle of heaven. I watch the clouds with their silver sails drift by, but within me there is the same tug, incessant, torturing, killing. . . .

I go to the theatre. I see the struggles of humanity portrayed—love, strife, joy, hate; but what is their pain to mine? Theirs closes with the drop of the curtain; mine goes on and on into the night, making of the day of life a darkness blackening all things as if with soot, clouding even the beautiful and the good.

I go to my friend. He tries to console me. "Arise, awake from this stupor. You are young; you have power. Will you stifle the soul that can shed radiance on all about it? Is life so long that you dare cast away its finest years?" I listen persistently, hoping that the voice too may hear and be silent. But the gnawing at my heart goes on.

I seek G-d. I pour forth my plaints; I uncover my sorrow, but He seems to say, "This is your problem, human; you alone must solve it. As you approach your solution, you draw near to Me." And there, too, I find no balsam for my troubled soul. Despair sets in. "Doomed you are, and doomed you shall remain!" That cry keeps ringing in my ears. Its resonance frightens me. It drives me wild with rage. "Stop, stop, you tom-tom of the heart, you vulture of the soul!" And I ask myself, "Will it always be thus? Is this to be the measure of my earthly existence? Dissatisfaction, despair, hopelessness?"

An idea strikes me. I have appealed to nature, to pleasure, to my friend, to my G-d. Fool, why not analyze the call of the voice? Why not seek within yourself? Like the break of dawn, when the rosy-fingered rays of the early morning sun rise up above the distant grayish horizon and bring light where darkness reigned before, so this thought takes hold of me. It storms my being, it sweeps from nerve to nerve, from fibre to fibre. Everything within me calls forth in anticipation. "Voice, what are you? What is the price of my freedom from bondage?" And then I hear a wonderful exposition of youthful thoughts and youthful fancies. It speaks of life, of love, of hope, of fame. . . . It speaks in soothing tones.

"The blood of youth flows with the uncontrollable force of a mountain stream, winding its way past every obstacle. It reflects the sunshine by day and mirrors the moon by night. At times it leaps precipitately downhill, and on short level stretches it winds calmly along; but always it is moving, coursing on. Why dam the driving stream that leads inevitably to the sea of hope? Why block up the flood whose fount is life, and whose mouth kisses the ocean's waves in the joyous union of consummation and fulfillment? Life calls, the race is on, whether to win or lose, yours to run."

And behold! Slowly my pain is eased. I am led back to my truer self—to my faith in life. The laurel is not for the swiftest, the wreath is not for the subtlest; but the crown of olives is surely for him who races with earnestness and sincerity.

II.

I was once walking along a country road with a friend. On all sides of us were nature's charms. A sudden turn of the road brought us near an apple tree laden with fruit. Under the tree stood a band of boys hurling rocks at its upper branches, and with every stone the apples fell and crashed to the ground, and not infrequently a branch came tearing down as a result of the barrage. I remarked to my friend, "Have you noticed that tall stately fir tree, how symmetrically it rises to the heavens? No stones mar its branches and none of its limbs are broken by damaging missiles. Thus has it always been, my friend; it is the fate of the trees that bear fruit to receive the blows of life, to have its fruit thrown to the ground, to have its branches broken and its outward form covered with bleeding bark where the jagged end of a rock has left its traces."

III.

The rivers are marching to the sea. The great trek is on. From the tiniest rivulet to the widest of majestic floods, all join in the pilgrimage to the sea. It is outing time for the inhabitants of water. They float along with the impulsion of the stream. They rest under rocks, and dart swiftly to the surface to mouth some stray floating morsel.

I sit by the bank of a tiny river and watch the parade to the sea. But more than speckled fish and slippery members of the piscary tribe are on their way. The flotsam and jetsam, cast into the waters by human hands, are tagging along in the great procession.

I hurl a tiny stone into the stream and watch the ripples it creates. The effect remains, but the stone has disappeared to the bottom. But the lighter driftwood flows on with the tide. Its very lightness is its salvation, for it successfully slides along over the surface and winds ultimately safe to the sea.

How true of the stream of life that carries on its crest that which is light and bears it to the sea of success, while that which is weighty sinks and drowns with but a few ripples to mark its grave.

IV.

Little Rebecca gazed wistfully out of the window. Her eyes were swollen from the tears that had poured from her heart, as the blood from a fresh wound. If she could only put the broken vase together again. It had seemed so pretty with its dainty little pictures and its colorful designs, perched out of the reach of her tiny hand. From the chair she had hoped to examine it at closer range. And now it lay on the floor dashed to pieces, and mother was angry.

Clouds, pregnant with rain, had been gathering. Drops of rain began to play a tattoo on the window. Rebecca watched the steady pitter patter with thoughtful interest. Her mother approached and put her arm about the child's shoulder. Rebecca raised her tear-filled eyes and said, "See, mother, G-d, too, is angry, for he weeps at my naughtiness."

SALMAGUNDI

By

HIRSCHEL E. REVEL

An essential component of the literature of every age is the recorded reflections about life, penned by courageous but slightly bewildered adolescents fast approaching adulthood and its concomitant social responsibilities. These reflections, from the Biblical narrative of young Isaac's implicit faith both in his father and in G-d, down to the well-meant effusions of the college magazines of our own day, are of extreme importance, inasmuch as they faithfully mirror the reactions of the young man to the system of standards and ideals upon which his education is based.

Yeshiva College is the fruition of a certain set of ideals, unique in the singlar beauty of its power and scope, fusing, as it does, Israel's perennial moral truths with the best in present-day scientific culture into one spiritually harmonious entity. As the influence of this Yeshiva College spirit can now be seen taking its first faltering steps, the opinion of one of its students as to the possibility of these ideals being eventually translated into pragmatic precepts which can be injected into the daily life of the American Orthodox Jew, should prove of interest. I do not, naturally, arrogate to myself the position of being a representative voice of the Yeshiva College student-body; I merely wish to present my individual views for what they may be worth.

Many, regarding the herculean task the Yeshiva College has set itself, the reconciliation and coalescence of two forces apparently antipodal in their disparity, consider the project impossible of achievement. For one whose acquaintanceship with the work of Yeshiva College is only second-hand, this view is entirely warranted, but one who has had the opportunity of familiarizing himself with its actual work, sees that in this case the seemingly impossible can become a living reality. Here we must stop to distinguish between outer syncretism

with its simulated external appearances, which is the path of least resistance, and inner synthesis rooted in uncompromising, unswerving belief capable of noble self-sacrifice, which is our true goal.

Immemorially, the college student has been the questioner, the doubter, the rebel—albeit, the pansophist. Leaders in education have usually wisely refrained from confining this spirit of investigation, realizing that time can be relied on to cool even the most inflamed ardor; and bitter experience has also taught them the futility of any attempt to clip the soaring wings of the bird of healthy inquisitiveness.

The perplexities of the college student of today are in direct proportion to the complexity of present-day life. Besides the eternal problems of theology and metaphysics which are, so to speak, an obstinate inheritance, there exist the more immediate, personal questions of love, a future, and religion—and now are superadded the doubts engendered by the imminent collapse of our over-vaunted capitalistic economic society.

We can, therefore, understand the plight of the Yeshiva College student, whose back must be broad enough to bear not only the problems of the average collegian, but also the increased burden of an entirely new group of problems which are the by-products of the mental and spiritual synthesis which I have mentioned.

Adulthood is the transitional period when youth's main occupation ceases to be preparing for, and becomes living, his life. The new-born infant, puzzled by the jumble of faces, sounds, colors, forms and other meaningless stimuli surrounding him; the baby, gleefully finding that his toes are controlled by him and can be sucked, pulled, or wiggled at will; the tot, momentously discovering that by certain maneuvers of his feet he can become self-propelling and thus explore the mysterious recesses of his nursery; the child, mastering the alphabet and the primer—which unfold to him new unending worlds of fascinating fact and fancy; the lad, learning family and social relationships; the stripling, preoccupied with games and sports, hunting and fishing; the pubescent, organizing in team-play, demanding loyalty and swearing fealty; the youth, with his dawning interest in biology, botany, and the marvels of Nature's secrets of re-creation; the ephebe, in hesitant, blushing cognizance of the charm and appeal of the other sex; the adolescent, mooning and moping, and his indiscriminate devoural of all depictions of life, accepting fiction, romances, and movies as true portraits; the young man, smarting from his first disillusioning taste of the ruthlessness and viciousness of life: all these afford us glimpses, and are single flashes, converging into one brilliant ray which directs itself at, and illumines in bold relief, the role that man's unquenchable thirst to amass knowledge and existence, plays on the stage of life.

The culminating point of these successive stages of knowledge-seeking is the typical college senior. It is just before graduation and he is pondering his life in retrospect. His intellect is cloyed with books—books in every language and of every description; folios, octavos, duodecimos; text-books, scientific books; books of history, travel, and adventure; books purporting to be psychological and philosophical, salacious books, books of drama and humor, books and more books, books . . . *ad nauseam*. Nothing blunts the edge of a sharp, keen, young mind more quickly and thoroughly than the bitter corrosion of indiscriminate factual knowledge. The printed word has long been to him a key wherewith to unlock the inviting portals of the entrancing palace which contains the treasured pleasures of life. Through the medium of the printed word, he has acquainted himself with the foibles and eccentricities of all creation. But, in a desperate endeavor to swallow, in a short period of time, all recorded knowledge of life, he has gorged himself and is suffering from acute mental indigestion. Books are not to blame for his condition; we must beware of the old fallacy,

post hoc, ergo propter hoc. Books are invaluable; they are the links of the onward march of civilization. Our college senior's mental satiety is rather to be explained by a peculiar state of mind of which over-consumption of reading matter is not a cause, but an expected consequence.

Let us probe deeper into the psychology of our college senior, who is tired of learning life and wants to live life. His trials and tribulations are numerous. At times he feels inextricably caught in the maelstrom of cruel fate. Let us pretend that our college senior, realizing our genuine sympathy with him in his manifold difficulties, has permitted himself to be coaxed into baring for us some of his misgivings and perplexities. In order to become better acquainted, we are introduced to him. We see an attractive chap, about twenty-one years of age, a well-knit five-foot ten, with curly hair, serious mien, clear, deep eyes twinkling good-naturedly on the slightest provocation, (and possessed of such other qualities as may appeal to the taste of the reader).

In the first place, (we hear him saying), although I rather dislike admitting it, I don't like people. Most of them are dull and commonplace, they seem completely satisfied leading a life which is one round after another of eating, sleeping, procreating, and finally dying. They go about their daily tasks with a deadening regularity and stultifying changelessness which remind me of the complacency of the normal animal chewing its cud in phlegmatic contentment until its allotted hour is up. These people have no impulsive yearning for the higher things of life; no spiritual cravings; no constantly onward-beckoning ideals; no driving desire to improve their lot; they stagnate serenely. Their existence is a progressive vegetation. Similarly, their conversation consists mainly of boring banalities liberally punctuated with such distinctive interjections as: "You don't say!"; "Aw, go on!"; "Who'd have ever dreamt it!"; "Isn't it just too darling (or just too cute) for words." It is safe to assume that this slovenly language is a sure indication of the paucity of the underlying thought substrata. Yet even the conversation of the middle and upper classes tends to be confined to small talk about business, politics, baseball, the weather, clothes, and the exchange of petty social amenities, all of which, although having a definite place, should not be the sole resources of conversation, to the exclusion of stimulating discussions of intellectual, artistic, and cultural topics, as is, regrettably, too often the case.

There is another group, he amplifies, whose obnoxiousness is entirely out of proportion to its actual number, and these are people who either do not have or do not care to use sufficient will-power to prevent their egotistic desires and crude cravings from rising to the surface of their unconscious, and overflowing into their every gesture and action and even from imprinting themselves in their very physiognomies. These are people capable of absorbing fulsome praise, people regarding their physical wants of supreme moment to everybody present, people who refuse to regulate the tenor of their conversation with regard to their listeners, people who fetishize food and turn dinner-tables into gastronomic marathons; in short, people who violate the elementary laws of convention and show an uncanny knack of persistently transgressing proprieties—whose sense of decorum is seemingly atrophied. I, of course, realize that self-gratification in its multitudinous disguises is the *deus ex machina* which prescribes the actions of us puppets, but humanity has long decreed, for mutual agreeableness, that certain too-common strivings shall not be placed on constant exhibition but shall be relegated to the privacy of the individual. This is the first theorem of social life; gentlemanliness, chivalry, and social nicety are its corollaries, and consequently anyone who declines to act in accordance with this world-wide and age-old ruling renders himself noxiously offensive. In this category I do not include the out-and-out narcissist, who is a subject for the psychiatrist, and excites only pity.

Even among my fellow students I find a disconcerting conglomeration of quidnuncs, votaries of sesquipedalian forensic eloquence, devout disciples of *Sitzfleisch*-impelled mentation, near-geniuses with unimposing, unimpressive exteriors; pleasant-faced dullards; bibliophiles, semi-psychopaths; bullet-headed athletes, pan-cynics with inferiority complexes; quasi-intellectuals disdaining life, sublimating in philosophical abstractions of it; fanatics of all sorts; balanced, thank goodness, by the backbone of the student-body, those essentially normal.

I now come to the question of my own psycho-sexual discretions, which I shall not discuss, although doubtless they would prove of interest; because should I start frankly, I am afraid embarrassment would soon embroil me in ingenious but fruitless tergiversations. (We fully understand and appreciate the stand of our college senior, and we will not press him to change his view).

Now, continues our college senior, I should like to voice a few objections with respect to college teaching and college curricula. Teachers can be divided into four classes: the inspired and inspiring; the inspired but uninspiring; the uninspired but inspiring; and the uninspired and uninspiring. I have spent many of the happiest hours of my intellectual life with teachers of the first type, but many more are the torturous, interminable hours I have wasted, day-dreaming under the soporific influence of monotonous droning tones emanating from representatives of the last division. Educators should be endowed with sufficient perspicuity to realize that education cannot and will not progress if teachers are expected to be mere machines dispensing knowledge upon the deposit of a certain sum in the automat of modern college-training. Teachers should not be weighed in the scales of text-book value; they should be chosen both for their knowledge of facts, and, what is more important, for their ability to imbue their students with a zest and love for knowledge. The curriculum of my college offers more than three-hundred courses of study of startling diversity, and it is the fond hope of the faculty that the subjects which the student assimilates during his four years at college will fall into step and conflate themselves into one harmony, commonly called a college-education, which will serve him as a guide to the art of successful living. Whether or not this transpires is highly problematical. With this rather trenchant observation, our college-senior concludes the airing of his views.

After having listened to the misgivings of the average college senior, let us turn our attention to that rara avis, the Yeshiva College senior. They are indeed rare, there being only fifteen in existence at the present writing, and as their rarity makes them reticent, we shall unfortunately not be able to persuade one of them to paint for us his feelings and position, and we must, perforce, continue our discussion with facts derived from other channels of knowledge.

The Yeshiva College senior is historically unique, he is the living proof of the theory advanced and maintained by certain far-sighted sages in present-day Israel, whose claim is that the truth of the Torah and the truth of Science are the two avenues of approach to eternal truth. The temptation to leave the expression "eternal truth" unexplained so as not to disturb its pristine euphony, is indeed great, but for the sake of lucidity we shall define it as a code of morality born of a scientific knowledge of the external world plus a deep understanding and appreciation of the abysmal profundities of human nature, and the happiness induced by living in accordance with it. The divine code of morality as enjoined in the Torah is a code of morality of eternal truth, which is strictly adhered to by the Torah-true Jew because of his unshakable belief in its divine wisdom, and only secondarily because his keen, innate sense of justice convinces him of the existence of a future world of reward and punishment. We thus see that the approach of the Torah to external truth consists in the insistence on the practise of an ennobling morality, and so firmly has the Torah imbued, inculcated, and ingrained tenets of high ethical value into countless generations of Jews, that moral virtues have penetrated and permeated their very lifeblood, until morality itself has become a visibly dynamic factor in the racial inheritance of the Jew. The approach of Science to external truth, however, takes the stand that morality is the apogee of all knowledge, and until man has reached and

scaled the summits of knowledge, morality is neither logically incumbent nor scientifically valid, although it is advisable for the sake of society.

Side by side with the moral injunctions of the Torah, there exists a very involved complex system of ritualistic commandments; both of these systems are of equal importance, for if one denies the divinity of one, he must deny the divinity of the other. To the uninitiated this mass of ritual seems to be an insufferable yoke around the neck of the observant Jew. This mistaken notion has obtained for centuries, and it is not realized that as the Jew believes with his heart and soul that the observance of these laws will gain him salvation, the heeding of them brings the greatest possible joy and pleasure.

The Yeshiva College seniors form the first generation of Orthodox Jewry who are meeting face to face the necessity of becoming equally conversant with two cultures, the glorious religious heritage of their fathers, and the stark, strident, scientific culture of today. They are the junction of the two onrushing torrents of mighty cultures; turbulent in them are the angry roar, the fierce swirling and splashing, the foaming spray, and the powerful counter-eddies and whirlpools which must inevitably precede the peaceful flow of two bodies of water as one. The Yeshiva College seniors are pioneers of the spirit, blazers of new trails, and must therefore undergo many trying hardships which cannot be eased or mitigated.

A few hundred years ago the world began to recognize its duty to its mentally disabled; some fifty years ago, the diseases of the unconscious mind were charted; twenty-five years ago the Mental Hygiene movement, which attempts to help those suffering from mental afflictions, had its inception. The next logical step is for an understanding movement, the aim of which is to keep the average college student whose troubles and perplexities I have touched upon, and who is seriously seeking enlightenment and guidance, from being overwhelmed by the constantly shifting standards and the precipitate mental fluxes of the present generation, which are threatening to engulf the weakest in depths of despair.

We can all testify, from either past or present experience, that youth is abnormally susceptible to the germs of pessimism and its multiple hydra-headed incarnations. Witness the suicide rate and the vogue of pseudo-Schopenhauerian cults in collegiate circles. No doubt, some day, Schopenhauer will get a long-deserved vote of apology from studentdom who have persistently perverted, obscured, and discredited his epoch-making philosophy.

· I have placed undue emphasis on the bleak, dreary side of the college student's life, but only for a purpose. In reality, there are certain pleasures of pure, surpassing exaltation which can be experienced only by carefree youth, and which cannot be repeated or recaptured in later life.

The indomitable truth-seeking spirit of Youth is a bulwark against which the waters of despondency dash themselves in vain. The college youth of the world are the heartbeats of civilization; dejection and despair are not their lot. With chin held high, armed with a supply of mild resignation, and with a brave and wholesome outlook, forged from his ideals, his soul-searchings, his joys and his sorrows, and tempered in the fire of intellectual honesty, the student can confidently proceed through life, respected by his fellow-men and becoming in the sight of G-d.

PRINCIPLES IN THE PHILOSOPHY OF HERMANN COHEN
(Continued from Page 46)

is our mission in the history of the world."

To summarize, the world is a logical system, not a mechanical order. All knowledge is based on the fundamental ideas. In logic, the derivative was found to lay the foundation for all mathematico-physical knowledge; in ethics, the idea of pure will reconciled all contradictions. The permanent relation of nature and ethics is assured by the idea of G-d,—that is, in the idea of truth which guarantees the possibility and ultimate realization of the ethical goal. The ethical self was conceived as the goal of totality which was continually approached, never completely realized. Religion arises in the painful consciousness of the sinner, who feels his retrogression from the ethical goal and despairs of ever reaching the ever-advancing army on the ethical road. Belief in G-d prevents the sinner from relapsing into despair and mysticism. It inspires him to act morally, thus starting him on the road of ethical progress.

This, in brief, is the outline of Cohen's philosophy, or at least my understanding of it. Owing to the practical impossibility of condensing the imposing edifice of Cohen's writings into an intelligle magazine article, the point of view herein presented will seem formal and far from convincing. Furthermore, systems based on reason and the rigorous analysis of mathematical logic commonly lack the plausibility that is popularly accorded to empirical philosophies. These disadvantages, however, should not blind us to the immense suggestive value of Cohen's approach. Philosophy is merely the organization of common knowledge, and the value of a philosophical system consists in the success with which it finds place for our various intellectual, æethetic, and moral values. From this point of view, Cohen's solution is well worth investigating. His works on the Jewish religion, too, though undoubtedly one-sided and too austerely logical, are yet replete with profound suggestions. The halls of the Torah are indeed spacious enough to include such diverse philosophies as the extreme rationalism of Hermann Cohen and the extreme mysticism of Martin Buber.

SHAKESPEARE—"TO BE OR NOT TO BE"
(Continued from Page 25)

really roam the Scottish highlands and cry out in Psalm-like ecstasy to the powers above, or was he merely the product of MacPherson's imagination? A cavalcade of these mysteries rides the range of our memory. . . . We pause to watch, we smile, and wish the searching scholars success.

STUDENTS' COUNCIL—(*Sitting l. to r.*) Aaron S. Feinerman, A Kellner, Hyman A. Israel, Abraham S. Guterman, Frank Hoffman. (*Standing l. to r.*) Jacob Karsh, William Kaufman, Morris Funk, Sidney Green, Meyer Greenberg, David Petergorsky, Harry Pelcowitz.

STUDENTS' COUNCIL

HYMAN A. ISRAEL—*President*

AARON DECTER—*V. Pres. (fall term)*   AARON KELLNER—*V. Pres. (spring term)*

FRANK HOFFMAN—Secretary

ABRAHAM S. GUTERMAN—*Editor*

•

CLASS OFFICERS

SENIOR CLASS
AARON S. FEINERMAN—*President*
SIDNEY GREEN—*V.* Pres.

JUNIOR CLASS
MORRIS FUNK—*President*
MEYER GREENBERG—*V.* Pres.

•

SOPHOMORE CLASS
DAVID PETERGORSKY—*President*
HARRY PELCOWITZ—*V.* Pres.

FRESHMAN CLASS
JACOB KARSH—*President*
WILLIAM KAUFMAN—*V.* Pres.

•

THE MAIN STEM

By

SAMUEL DEUTSCH

Life, they say, is a chronic sickness from which ten out of ten die. In Times Square, known as the Main Stem, life is merely a series of striking events. Taste it once, and you enjoy it. Too often, it cloys the appetite.

Times Square at night. The heart of New York ablaze. The world's playground. Windows flashing with jewelry, perfumes, costumes, pictures; waving masses of people in gaudy uniforms or more gaudy gowns; arc-lights, quivering red and blue, shading their simmering rays on the ever-continuous swarms of passersby. Tides of people chattering, murmuring, shuffling; streams of motors clashing, hooting, bellowing; cafés, tea-rooms sparkling,—and a pale mild moon, seemingly out of place, calmly sailing above the din of Times Square.

The street of wrecked romances. The most noted thoroughfare in the world. The mirror of a metropolis and a nation. The heart of New York —and the world. Stand on the corner and look at life. Then cast yourself into the stream and flow along.

A few faces peer out spectrally from the never-ceasing stream; the dandy, the loafer, the banker, the peddler, the actress. A "newsie" rushes to deliver his wares. And that man trying to sell his apples to the fleeting crowd. That tot, over there, is evidently lost. But move on.

There is the Rivoli. The word Rivoli is ablaze in all its glory. Myriads of lights. A streaming announcement. "You must come in. See the best show in town."

But you can't pause here long. You must keep moving. Moving. You must keep time to the rhythm of shuffling feet. You cannot lag behind. You go further. Again you are drawn into the maelstrom.

This is the Astor. A swanky place. No cloaks' operator can go in here. That is, if he wants to hold on to his pay. The door is open. A flurry of insane laughter. You have passed.

There is the Hollywood Restaurant, which is no restaurant. It is a night club. The name sounds better, you see. In hard times, they give free meals to the unemployed. Charitable. You've probably heard of the Hollywood. One of the "better" night clubs in the town. The most beautiful girls. . . .

This is a hotel. It says so in front in silvered letters. Outside, you pause and read a notice: "Apartments Available." On the East Side, it's just "Rooms to-let." Here it's "Apartments Available."

This restaurant over on this side, decorated to resemble a "Ye Olde Englishe Inn," is filled with diners. The better kind. Get a passing glimpse. Your glance falls on a couple. They're sitting at a table and conversing. Probably lovers. You look at the feminine part of the picture. She is a perfect forty despite her purchased beauty. The other member of the party of two—a perfect twenty, despite his being dressed up to look older.

He's a college fellow. He is now earning his living. She, a society lady with a lot of leisure time on her hands. Her husband's probably in bed, tired after a day in the office. She must have her good time. Money doesn't matter. And so, they're a "couple" for tonight.

This is Lindy's restaurant. Struck the front pages a couple of years ago. Was frequented by Arnold Rothstein. From here, Rothstein was called on the phone to receive a few "slugs" as a present from those who didn't quite admire him. Rothstein took himself for a walk instead of their taking him for a ride. The guilty one (or ones) has not as yet been found. A police commissioner resigned. A police shakeup ensued—the murder took place in Times Square. Quite a busy thoroughfare.

That, over there, is the Palace. A vaudeville house. It was different. Has been the dream of every "trouper." Ask any vaudeville actor his ambition, and the ready reply: "To hit the Palace." Now it has gone the way of all flesh. It is a movie house like the rest of them.

What's that crowd over there? An accident? No. It is a first night. A new play is having its opening tonight. Two new shows are folding up this very night. They have stayed for only a week. Perhaps this one will have more luck.

The crowd of first-nighters is on time. Old friends meet. New friendships are made. Congratulations are offered. A show for the common people. $6.60 for orchestra, twelfth row, side. "Step right this way, please."

A sweets shop. Rather strange, a store to sell cakes, pastries and even ordinary commonplace bread on Times Square. No . . . it isn't really a store. It is a charity bazaar. Sponsored by a "Ladies Society." "Come in and taste our cakes. Pay as much as you like."—A stout lady stands guard and with piercing eyes looks at the money plate—. Yes. Pay as much as you like.

"Good bread. We 'knead' the 'dough'."

Pretty considerate these society ladies are. Funds will be used to buy woolen coverings for the puppies whose owners can't afford to buy them. Dogs are beings, too. An act of charity is being performed on Times Square.

This is a book store. "Join a Book-of-the-Month club and give yourself an education" is their slogan. Good books. Best of literature. "Bad Girl." "Night Nurse." Get them here.

Books are displayed all over the show window. In the corner, a dusty "Shakespeare." Fix your glasses—you may notice it.

This 3-story building is a music publishing house. The latest hit from Tin Pan Alley may be procured here. Sounds of someone straining his vocal chords upstairs are caught by the attentive ear. There's a display window. Buy the latest songs direct from the publisher. Lots of songs. If you're a vaudeville actor, buy your ballads here. Just look at the titles: "I'm Just A Little Dandruff Trying To Get A-Head" or "Walking Through The Woods With a Male Chorus." Buy here and get good music. Special reduction. . . .

A street philosopher is trying to sell his wares. Weighs about 300 pounds, and is selling you something that will make you reduce. "Or your money back," he assures you. He speaks to the little crowd assembled near him, "The Democrats say the Republicans are wrong. The Republicans say the Democrats are wrong. I think they're both right. They're both wrong." The crowd smiles.

A new dispenser of wares pops up. He puts up his portable show and attracts the crowd. They gather around him. He sells his wares, too. Both peddlers are doing a flourishing trade. A cop appears. They disappear.

And now cast your eyes upward, although they begin to hurt a bit from the dazzling lights. Don't miss this sight—Times Square above the level of the street. News flashes from the Times building: flood in Ohio, gunman shot, Japan moves southward.

But perhaps you want to rest a bit. Allright, step right over this way, away from the scurrying of feet. Rest. But you can't—you have to listen to Times Square talk. You can't help listening.

It is full of weird sounds. Its voice is heartless and cold. The clatter of its vehicles and surface cars among the canyon-forming structures has an effect upon you. Automobile horns have a piercing, shrilling note, terribly distressing. The screech of the brakes as the traffic light turns red, jars on your nerves. You can't bear just to stand idly. You can't rest. You want to keep on moving. And you do keep on moving. You are caught in the spirit of Times Square.

Again you move into the line to mingle with the promenaders, all—you seem to think—wearing an inscrutably fatalistic mien, an expression of "I hope I get there in time." You, too, now walk with the same expression. You are no longer impressed as you were before you took that brief rest. You see throngs of people of all nationalities and creeds mingled in a feverish goallessness. You have become one of the crowd.

The lavishness, the brilliance, the "who cares?" of it all, now smite you with a fancy that you are sliding along to a soft, sickening melody. You drift. You have become merely a body moving with the tide.

And you are weary. You have seen enough for tonight. The scenes have induced a state of mental intoxication, and you just move along.

The dazzling lights produce a drowsiness. You have seen enough for tonight. You've seen the Main Stem.

You hurry along like the rest of them. You race towards home where it's quiet, peaceful and less turbulent. You go home, shutting off instinctively the hideous kaleidescope. You have tasted Times Square—from the outside.

PROMETHEUS OR TANTALUS?

(Continued from Page 20)

ing passage of his *Nouvelle Héloïse,* . . . "Think of Julie walking with her husband; the one admiring in the rich and splendid robe of the earth, the handiwork and the bounteous gifts of the author of the universe; the other seeing in it all nothing save a fortuitous combination, the product of blind force. Alas! she cries, the great spectacle of nature, for us so glorious, so animated, is dead in the eyes of Wolmar (Rousseau has Holbach in mind) and in that harmony of being, where all speaks of G-d in accents so mild and so persuasive, he only perceives eternal silence." Rousseau thus restored man to the privileged position from which he had been driven by the hardness of rationalism and the dreariness of atheism. With Rousseau and the romanticism which he set into action, the kingdom of heaven relapsed into the bosom of nature.

Psychogenetically, idealism is romanticism translated into a pseudo-rational logomachy, for is not idealism a philosophy of compensation? Man, again, is the center of the universe, for it exists only in his consciousness. Idealism compressed the universe into an atom and set it in the mind of man. Copernican astronomy reduced man to insignificance, but idealism replaced him upon his throne of eminence.

Modern philosophy reveals a constant oscillation

between rationalism and idealism. Schelling's romantic philosophy follows Hegel's dialectic. Schopenhauer's indefinable will follows closely upon Bentham's effort to construct a felicific calculus to measure human pleasure and pain. DuBois-Raymond's rationalism is later followed by Bergson's *élan vital.* Even pragmatism is compensatory in nature, for does it not surrender truth to human inhibitions by identifying the true and the useful? The illustrations are legion, and further enumeration is unnecessary.

Is man, then, condemned to constant oscillation between reason and illusion? Shall man ever stay his steps on the threshold of the dim temple of the Unknowable, and humbly whisper that terrifying word *Ignorabimus?* The answer is difficult. Yet, historical considerations seem to force the conclusion that man is by nature the embodiment of imagination and reason, of winged passions and slow-moving thought, of kaleidoscopic phantasies and colorless verities—in a word, an intersection of contraries. Like an island-universe afloat in the dreary realms of space, he is affected by the innumerable forces which he encounters in the inevitable course of his existence. Man is condemned to divine joy and to sad disenchantment. Man is a Prometheus in aspiration, but a Tantalus in accomplishment.

GERMANY AND THE JEWISH QUESTION

(*Continued from Page 34*)

censed masses. Like a wild beast, released from long captivity, the first taste of blood has not satiated their thirst but intensified their longing for more. The Nazi-army, more than a million strong, is delirious with its "victory" over helpless men, women, and children, and visualizes the dawn of a new era when Germany will rule supreme.

On the other hand, the changes wrought in the psychology of the German people hold little promise for a return of Germany to her pre-war culture. Unlike university students in other countries, the German student enters the university with an almost settled philosophy of life. The university only provides him with the scientific material which he needs for the perfection of his pre-conceived ideologies. And it is from this group that the future teachers, judges, prosecutors, government employees, and leaders in business will be drafted. The poison of racial hatred inculcated into their minds during the preceding years will not be eradicated for a long time to come. German culture has sunk to the level of the Middle-Ages and there is little hope that it can be resurrected before many decades will pass.

Similarly gloomy is the picture which the future has in store for German Jewry. The wounds inflicted during the last few years will require a long time for healing. Twenty years of intense suffering and economic deprivations and upheavals have robbed the Jewish youth of Germany of most of the characteristics which gained world-wide respect for German Jews. The young generation of Jews in Germany has never been young and resilient. It shared the economic hardships with the non-Jewish youth of Germany and, in addition, has been mentally broken by the anti-Semitic wave. It has never been prepared for the onslaught and has crumbled helplessly when the crisis came. Thousands of young Jewish men and women, whose contact with Judaism has always been very loose, are now looking toward Palestine as their haven of refuge. But it is a crushed and desperate group which now longs for the land of their ancestors. Many of them have already left the country of their birth and find joy and happiness on the soil in the land of "milk and honey." It is to be hoped that world opinion will make possible an easier lot for the Jews in Germany and that Palestine will open its doors to those who wish to escape from this land of darkness and intolerance.

EPITAPH

What? Is it lamentation that I hear?
Some one has died? Come, let me dry the tear
That makes your beauty maculate.
Come, let us laugh—or let us try to smile,—
What's one who's gone along the steep defile
That is with death commensurate?
Smile,—only smile. He wearied and went.
He hated life and was on death intent,

And so, unnoticed, slipped away.
He left a heart behind; behold his heart!
See, it is wounded by a poisoned dart
Which did his other woes outweigh.
How still he lies—a smile upon his lips
As with gold scissors Fate his life-thread snips!
At least this once he did not fail:
He wearied—and death calmed life's raging gale.

—Bernard Dov Millans

HUMOR

Cracks in Yeshiva Walls

"Fetchy" Friedman: Hey, waiter, another portion of meat.

Fine: "Don't you know any limits?"

"Fetchy": It's strange—when I'm at home in Providence, I don't eat much.

Fine: Only Providence can restrain your appetite.

.   *

"Chink" Feinerman, the political boss of the College, has been heard singing a new song, entitled: "Here Comes the Bribe."

*   *   *

Professor: Mr. Agushewitz, what is *creatio ex nihilo?*

Agush: A rabbi's sermon.

*   *   *

. . . . and there was "Schnozzle" Durante, the only man in the world who could smoke a cigar under a shower.

.   .   ..

To Hirschel Revel, on his receipt of a gold medal for proficiency in Jewish bibliography:

A wise man is he who knows his books from cover to cover. A wiser man is he who knows his books from title-page to title-page.

*   *   *

"A chiropodist," says Brandie (dere!), "is the lowest of professionals—he is constantly at your feet."

..   ..

"An idealist," says Norman Revel, "is a man who does good without himself benefitting materially from it—in plain words, a good-for-nothing."

Hoffman, the heavy-weight of the Yeshiva, was heard singing the song: "I Ain't Got Nobody."

*   *   *

Aaron Deeter, the Billy "Saturday" of the Yeshiva, has been advised that

"A sermon a day
Keeps the people away."

*   *   *

Hy Israel, our president, is to be engaged in social research. We are glad to publish his first work on the life of proletariat:

"I walked down Times Square, and saw a large number of women waiting for the Paramount to open. A half-hour later, I saw a great number of men standing in line on the Bowery to get their breakfast. Indeed, if the women are trying to get into the theatre so early in the morning, where else can the men get their breakfast?"

*   *   *

The Germans claim that the Jews are not being persecuted, but let us remember—*auf dem ga-nef brennt der Hitler.*

*   .

"The sophomores," said a professor, "are great book-lovers—especially during examinations."

*   *   *

Abie: Ask-your-wits, why do you pay only half-fare on the railroad?

Ask-your-wits: You see, I believe in the doctrine of predestination. By predestination is meant being at your destination before you start, and therefore I should pay no fare. But the company officials are atheists, and so they compromised with me for only half-fare.

ODE OF AN EVOLUTIONIST

Once I was a fish
And caught my worms with mirth,
But now I am a better dish
For Wall Street sharks on earth.

Once I was a frog
And by the swamps I skipped,
But now I'm in the bog
Because the banks have gypped.

Hail to thee, O noble Progress!
I worship only thee!
Don't ever reverse the process
And make a monkey of me.

SCHOOL ACTIVITIES

PRESIDENT'S MESSAGE

The past scholastic year has been one of rush and hurry for the Students' Organization. Unforseen events cut short our available extra hours and the result has been that the Students' Organization has had to forego certain quite necessary activities, notably students' assemblies.

In spite of the shortage of time, however, the Students' Organization has made certain definite forward strides in its efforts to create a higher coordination in the student body. Strict collection of fees at registration placed our treasury in better position to cope with students' needs. Under the care of a very efficient library staff, the Students' Library has doubled the number of books on its shelves, and has organized its circulation in such a way as to be of greater service to an increasing number of students. The Chess Club, a new organization in our school, has already won for itself a place in inter-collegiate chess circles. Our athletic organizations have maintained their usual activity and have called forth the usual interest and support. In spite of the present economic depression and a rather negligible interest manifested in certain student circles toward the students' publication, the *MASMID* promises to be bigger and better than it has ever been before. The Students' Organization has set a worthy precedent, we believe, in assuming leadership in the students' march on the occasion of the protest meeting against the German atrocities.

In viewing the future, we would recommend a more careful advance planning of students' activities. Well organized students' assemblies are essential to the greater unification of the student body, and we would urge that such assemblies be incorporated as an integral part of the school's calendar. Finally, we would call the attention of future administrations to the principle that the well-being and repute of the Students' Organization and of the school must at all times take precedence over the convenience of any individuals within the Organization, for only thus can the prestige of the institution be maintained in the eyes of the world as well as in the opinion of the students themselves.

HYMAN A. ISRAEL
President,
YESHIVA COLLEGE
STUDENTS' ORGANIZATION

SCHOOL NEWS
●
CHESS CLUB

The avtivities of the Chess Club during the past year are of especial significance, for they mark the first time Yeshiva College has engaged in an inter-collegiate tournament. Despite its lack of experience and insufficient preparation, the Yeshiva College Chess Team had a surprisingly successful debut, and succeeded in administering defeats to Brown University, University of Pittsburgh, and St. John's College. The team ranked fifth in the tournament, and the metropolitan press commented on its creditable showing. The team consisted of: Bernard Dov Milians, Philip Raymon, Israel Mowshowitz, and Harry Polachek, with Hirschel Revel and Samuel Tabak as substitutes. As we go to press, the team has issued a challenge to the Chess Club of Brooklyn College.

The success of the team spurred the Chess Club on to greater activity. It tendered an invitation to Charles Jaffee, world-renowned chess expert, who delivered a brilliant lecture on the Scotch Gambit, followed by a simultaneous match. The Club has also arranged a tournament to determine the team which is to represent the College during the next year.

PROTEST DEMONSTRATIONS

Yeshiva College, true to its ideal of leadership in Jewish life, played a notable part in the protest demonstrations against the atrocities of Hitlerism. The College was represented at the meetings of the American Jewish Congress, and collaborated with it in arranging protest meetings and demonstrations. In connection with the huge Madison Square Garden mass meeting on the 27th of March, Yeshiva College organized a parade of the college youth of New York. A call was issued to the metropolitan colleges, and the students, both Jew and Gentile, responded eagerly. The representatives of practically every college in the city assembled at 59th Street, starting point of the parade, under their respective college banners. With the blue and white banner of Yeshiva College in the van, the students marched impressively to the Garden, where a section had been reserved for them. The voice of Yeshiva College mingled with the mighty voice of protest which the assembled thousands thundered across the sea.

The spirit of Yeshiva College again manifested itself on May 10th when the student body asked—almost demanded—that they be allowed to sacrifice their Field Day to be able to participate in the anti-Hitler parade. And once again Yeshiva College led the student groups. The parade was a memorable event. The thousands of marchers and the cheering thousands, massed along the sidewalks, were evidence of the fact that American Jewry and American Jewish youth no longer considered prayer to be their only weapon. The spontaneity of spirit and enthusiasm, shown by students of Yeshiva College, gives the lie to the charge that American Jewish youth is sluggish and apathetic. They showed that they were imbued with an active, dynamic spirit. They would no longer suffer meekly and passively. Their cry is "Action!" The boys observed the fast day decreed by the Union of Orthodox Rabbis of the United States and Canada, solemnly and religiously, but in addition they lifted their voices in loud and vigorous protest.

SPORT SHOTS

An unusually strong support of athletics was shown during the 1932-33 season. There were encouraging signs of an awakened interest in the various sports and all indications point to an increasing zeal on the part of the student body for the advancement of our Alma Mater in intercollegiate competition. The reception of the newly innovated intra-mural programs also promises much for the future of this department of extra-curricular activity.

BASKETBALL NEWS

Though without the usual fanfare that accompanies the opening of a college athletic season, the call for basketball candidates was answered enthusiastically. From a large turnout a squad of 10 men was picked and practice sessions held regularly. The ranks of the varsity, depleted by graduations, were filled mostly by freshmen and the schedule was begun with lots of pep. As usual it included clubs, schools and community centers. In spite of handicaps resulting from lack of time and practice, the team piled up enough victories for a 5 game winning streak, finally losing to our old rivals, the Church of Our Saviours Atonement, but atoned for this by defeating them in a hard fought return game. A game and dance were arranged in conjunction with the Young Israel of Tremont, and an enjoyable evening was had by all. At midyear we lost two of our regulars who transferred to other schools, but fighting spirit carried us on to several more wins.

After the last game the team elected Hy Aronoff to the captaincy of 1933-34. Numerals were awarded to varsity men at the close of the season.

The names of the team members follow: Morris Gordon, Israel Friedman, Hy Aronoff, Al Troy, Dave Fallek, Tsvi Brown, Lou Muss, "Red" Kasten, Sid Green (Captain).

In general basketball always appeals most to our students and we look to have still more improvement in our next season.

BASEBALL

Little emphasis was placed on baseball this year due to the pressure of studies. However, a varsity was picked to represent the school and several practices were held. The college scored an easy victory over the Talmudical Academy, but its game with the S. O. Y. was called on account of rain. Several intra-mural contests resulted in wins for the lower classes. As we go to print, we have games on our schedule with the Torrens Club, the Olins A. C. and a final game with the S. O. Y.

An attempt was made to arouse interest in track and field events, but though a creditable response was given and the services of a coach enlisted, it was necessary to postpone our debut in intercollegiate track until next year.

Yeshiva College Students Library

Until this year, a well-developed Library was the hope and prayer of the rank and file of the student body, while the politicians could always fall back upon the topic of Library development whenever they wanted to rudely jar the lethargy of the Students' Council, and, at the same time, exhibit their school spirit. It was, therefore, with cynical incredulity that the school heard that the Library was being reorganized and its scope widened. At first the enterprising Librarian, Mr. Isaac Goldberg, met quizzically good-natured smiles when he requested some measure of co-operation from the political bosses of the school. This attitude was pardonable because for four years the Library had announced prospective enlargement without doing anything about it.

With unquenchable determination and vigor and almost single-handedly, Mr. Goldberg began a task of transformation which he carried to a very successful conclusion. As soon as he had infused into the Library some spirit of life, the Students' Council sat up and took notice, and greatly facilitated his work by granting him large (relatively speaking) sums of money. With the able assistance of Mr. Leo Judah Usdan, Mr. Goldberg proceeded to install modern library facilities and equipment, and then, from various sources, he gathered a fine collection of indispensable books. He informs us that his statistics show that the circulation of books during the past seven months of his incumbency exceeds the eight hundred mark, and the number of those using the reference department exceeds three thousand. His catalogue, completely indexed and thoroughly cross-indexed as it is, and his library systems are a delight to even the most exacting Librarian. It is our hope that the Librarians of future years will possess the same devotion to the Library and give the College as good service as Mr. Goldberg has rendered us this year.

The Unending Quest

The multicolored vestments gay,
  The cloak that mother Nature wore,
The verdant leaves in rich array,
  To me but sombre sorrow bore.

        I yearned to find the secret door
          Wherein content and joy abound;
        Wherein I might with peace explore
          The riddle of this earthly round.

              I sought the truths of ancient tomes
                That bore the majesty of time,
              They spoke of high celestial domes,
                And angels' song in sacred rhyme.

                    They told of joy, of peace, and rest,
                      Of bliss in union with the Power,
                    That makes and guides, at his behest,
                      The world, entwined in trouble's bower.

                        What boots, thought I, of joy to treat
                          That follows on our journey sad;
                        To race on glass with naked feet
                          Is no way soothed by goal so glad.

                            When key I found there was no door,
                              When door appeared, where fled the key?
                            What lies beyond and what before,
                              Was locked in all eternity..

I sought aloft through heaven's course
  The fount of light of moon and sun,
The very gleam obscured the source,
  And light was dark—ah what strange fun!

    A peeping bud I pondered long;
      It burst—behold a flower fair!
    Whence came this beauty like a song
      To charm the soul, with colors rare?

        But short, its colors gone, I find
          Its petals dried, it droops its head.
        Alas what joy the careless wind
          Has brought to fall, in silence, dead.

            A cripple struck my saddened view
              His eyes bespoke the pain of life
            His pangs were great, his pleasures few,
              Deformed, he faced this world of strife.

                His eyes flamed words by passion fired
                  " 'Tis chance and chance alone that rules"
                In vain to climb, to have aspired
                  If stroke of nature ardor cools.

                    When key I found, there was no door,
                      When door appeared, where fled the key?
                    What lies beyond and what before,
                      Was locked in all eternity.

The First Modern Talmud Torah

By

· Isaac Goldberg

In these days of educational achievement and application of scientific method to the working-out of curricula in our Hebrew schools, it is interesting to turn back the pages of the history of Jewish education, and see for ourselves from what source developed our so-called advanced educational program.

About two hundred and fifty years ago, in 1680 to be exact, there appeared in Amsterdam, a name frequently met with in the annals of Jewi-h history, a work, the importance of which to Jewish bibliography cannot be overestimated—I refer to the *Sifthe Yeshenim* of Shabbethai Meshorer Bass, the father of Jewish bibliography. The book is of great importance, listing as it does all the known printed Hebrew books extant in the compiler's day, their contents, their authors, date and place of publication, and their sizes. We think, however, that the importance of this book is over-exaggerated in contrast with the lack of general interest shown in his preface to the work. It is here that he outlines for us, (the first of its kind), the first progressive curriculum of the Talmud Torah of Amsterdam. This Talmud Torah has a further interest for us, for it was the first Jewish educational institution where Jewish children could get a well rounded-out Jewish education.

Following is an excerpt from the preface to the *Sifthe Yeshenim*: "The Talmud Torah is a separate edifice housing six large rooms. To each one there was assigned an instructor, a highly-trained man and a specialist in his field. Children remain in the first class until they have learned to read their prayers. In the second class they are taught Scripture, with the peculiar chant of the Sefardic Jews; they remain here until they have become versatile in Bible. Upon entering the third class, they are taught to explain and translate the Bible into their own tongue (Spanish); they cover the weekly portion of the Torah, concentrating on Rashi's commentary. The Prophets and Hagiographa are taught in the fourth class. The method of instruction was as follows: one pupil would read a passage in Hebrew, explaining it in Spanish. The other children had to be attentive, for each was called upon in turn. In the fifth class they are taught to accustom themselves to read *Halacha* (Mishna) until they had attained the understanding and insight required of a *"Bachur"*.* The only language spoken in this class was Hebrew; they used Spanish to translate and explain the *Halacha*. Here, too, grammar was taught. They were in the habit of learning one *Halacha* (one legal chapter of the *Cemara*) everyday. Before a festival, however, all the students learned the appropriate portion of the *Shulchan 'Arukh*, until they had become well-versed in the regulations of that holiday. Students who have successfully passed through these five classes now enter the last class, the sixth—the *Yeshiva* of the *beth hamedrash*,—where they are under the personal supervision of the Chief Rabbi. Daily they study here on *halacha* with the detailed comments of Rashi and the Tosafoth, and dispute diligently the decisions of Maimonides, Rabbi Jacob ben Asher, Rabbi Joseph Caro (author of the *Beth Jo:eph*), and other codifiers. For the use of these advanced students there was organized a large and well-stocked library, from which they can borrow books only for reference in the school; not even for the deposit of a large sum of money was a book lent out of the building.

The hours of learning were the same for all classes; from eight until eleven o'clock in the morn-

---

* The Jewish conception of *"Bachur"* can be compared to that of the medieval baccalaureus who, with his baccalaureate degree, could pursue higher studies.

ing, and from two until five o'clock in the afternoon. In the winter, the afternoon session was prolonged until the time for evening prayers. . . . Every *paterfamilias* had a tutor to review the lessons with the child, to teach him to write Spanish and Hebrew, and also to instruct him in the art of versification. . . . The instructors were chosen by the community, and each one was paid from the Talmud Torah treasury according to his worth, needs, and services. No teacher was forced to flatter parents or students (something indulged in today by our Jewish Hebrew school teachers) ; they taught all alike—poor and rich received the same measure of attention."

The curriculum outlined above is very important for us, being in use in the first modern Talmud Torah. This school became distinguished for scholarship and produced some of our most notable Jews, among others Spinoza and Menasseh ben Israel.

THE SECOND GENERATION

(Continued from Page 39)

ican Jews. In solving these problems, we shall be laying the foundation for an American Jewish community. We shall not lose our identity. Our past holds us too strongly, and our present renders straying uncomfortable. Our life may be different than that of our Palestinian brethren, but that will mean nothing more than that they are living in Palestine and we in America."

Hartman remembers his feelings when his son had finished speaking. He recalls that he felt the entire foundation of his life being gently but firmly removed from under him. The calm relativism of his son was shattering beliefs and hopes which had served as bulwarks of his inner being. His ideals of a free Jewish nation living on its ancient soil would not be realized, as he had hoped, in the lives of his own grand-children. The Hebrew tongue which for him was holy would at best be but a secondary language on their lips. And the age-old persecutions—would they strike low his American descendants, as they had stricken the Jews of every land under the sun?

Hours pass, the moon sinks behind the western horizon, the music has ceased, and the lovers are no longer to be seen at the railing. In the light of the dawn, the faintly visible outline of the hills can be made out in the distance—the hills of which Hartman had dreamed, and which he had longed to inhabit. But the sight of these hills does not call forth a joyous light from expectant eyes. Wearied by his painful thoughts and feelings, Hartman has sunk into a fitful sleep.

Co pli ents of

Harry Fishel

Co pli ents of

Mendel Gottesman

Compliments of

Roggen Bros. & Co., Inc.

Co? pli? ents of

Louis Gold

Co ı pli ı ents of

HENRY FEUERSTEIN
FAMILY

HENRY FEUERSTEIN & FAMILY

SAMUEL C. FEUERSTEIN & FAMILY

VICTOR FEUERSTEIN & FAMILY

HAROLD FEUERSTEIN & FAMILY

MAX COHEN & FAMILY

Compliments of

MR. & MRS.
JACK RABINOWITZ

BOSTON, MASS.

Compliments of

MR. & MRS. SAUL BERMAN

BOSTON, MASS.

Compliments of

MR. & MRS.
VICTOR FEUERSTEIN

Compliments of

MR. & MRS. MORRIS USDAN

Compliments of

MR. & MRS. B. J. KAPLAN

BROOKLINE, MASS.

Co₁pli₁ents of

Imperial Manufacturing Co.

524 Broadway, New York, N. Y.

Co₁pli₁ents of

Mr. & Mrs. Morris Usdan

IN MEMORY

OF

MORRIS HAUSMAN

THE PERFECT THREAD CO.

Max Usdan, *Prop.*

39 WEST 19th STREET

NEW YORK

Lightning Source UK Ltd.
Milton Keynes UK
UKHW021133090219
336936UK00008B/1154/P